Your Child from 5 to 11

Margaret McSpedden

BAY BOOKS
Sydney and London

This book is copyright. Apart from any fair dealing for the purpose of private study, research, criticism or review, as permitted under the Copyright Act, no part may be reproduced by any process without written permission. Enquiries should be addressed to the publisher.

Published by Bay Books
61-69 Anzac Parade,
Kensington NSW 2033.

Publisher: George Barber
Copyright Margaret McSpedden

National Library of Australia
Card Number and ISBN 1 86256 286 5

BB 88
Printed in Singapore

CONTENTS

INTRODUCTION 5

1. **THE AGES AND STAGES OF GROWTH**
   An outline of the development that occurs during each of the primary-school years 9

2. **AND SO TO SCHOOL**
   How to help your children before, during and after they start school 36

3. **GIRLS VERSUS BOYS: WHAT'S SEX GOT TO DO WITH IT?**
   Are the differences between girls and boys important? 48

4. **SPARE THE ROD AND SPOIL THE CHILD?**
   Ways of disciplining your children during their primary years 55

5. **"I'M BORED": FUN AND GAMES FOR EVERYONE**
   Activities that are enjoyed by children in the primary-school years 64

6. **YOU'VE GOT TO HAVE FRIENDS**
   Friends are very important to children in middle childhood 75

7. **GIVE YOUR KID A SPORTING CHANCE**
   Sport is a great interest and outlet for kids 83

8. **TELEVISION, VIDEOS AND COMPUTERS**
   Let's look at the influence of electronic media on our children 98

9. **HOW TO COPE WITH SOME OF LIFE'S LITTLE DIFFICULTIES**
   Some of the common problems faced by children in the primary years and how to cope with them 108

10. **FACING THE TEENS**
    How to prepare for the next stage 118

INTRODUCTION

I expect that you are reading this book because you are a parent of an under twelve or because you are somehow interested in children of this age group. So am I, and that is what has encouraged me to write this book. As the mother of two children under twelve, I tend to go from feeling guilty that I'm not doing enough to believing that they will survive anyway. Benign neglect is probably a better environment to grow up in than overwrought anxiety and pressure.

Parents often wonder what they can expect of their offspring during these important and enjoyable years of their life. With the trend to smaller families, parents are now more worried than ever about the one or two that they have. The problem is that by the time you have learned from your mistakes it's too late; they've grown up.

As a concerned parent, I looked for a book that could help me but found very little of real value. There are lots of books on childbirth and infancy, which you have probably already ploughed through, but little on children between five and eleven. At most, they rate a chapter in general books that have already devoted a chapter per month for new-borns. Surely something happens after they go to school and before they erupt into adolescence.

So, in this book we will look at these wonderful years as children develop in their level of understanding and independence. It is great fun being able to discuss the intricacies of life with them and watch the way they explain it all. Each age has its own rewards and its own difficulties.

By the time you have learned from your mistakes it's too late; they've grown up

> *"Mum, why is Jodie afraid of the lift?"*
>
> *"Because she was caught in one once."*
>
> *"But didn't she know there is a phone?"*
>
> *"Maybe she didn't know what it was for. Who would you ring if you were caught?"*
>
> *"I'd ring the fixer so they could come and get me out."*
>
> *Not bad for someone who's only five.*

In spite of the lack of books about them, children in this age group have delighted their parents for ages. Maybe that is why they have attracted so little attention; they are so interesting to be with that parents sought little help.

Nowadays, however, parents are more aware and more concerned about their children and how they should care for them. It is best to remove the idea of *should*, since it implies that there is only one way and that it fits all children and their parents. You are all individuals, as are your offspring, and you know best, so I suggest you temper everything in this book with the intimate knowledge you have of your own children.

In our society there seem to be more issues that worry parents bringing up their children than there were in the past. The influence of television, for example, has been much debated. Yet most kids watch television while their parents worry about whether they should, or how much is too much.

As well, there seem to be many more dangers in our society — unemployment, drug abuse, increasing crime and violence, and so on. Parents don't want their children to grow up to become unemployed drug addicts who have to steal to survive, and yet these unfortunates are somebody's children. If you have a clearer understanding of what to expect from your child during these important early years of their lives you will be better able to guide them down the right path. It may also make the job a little easier if you can understand the role of friends in your children's lives, how to help them with school, how to discipline them, and which sports may be best.

Unemployed drug addicts are somebody's children

While you will not expect Johnny to be still sucking his thumb at eighteen, at eight he may. And if such behaviour does not really upset you or your child, then just ignore the advice of well-meaning relatives or friends with "superkids". It is amazing how the comments of Aunt Jane can make an issue out of something, like having a light on during the night, which may undo all the good work you have done in getting your child to bed earlier.

> "You act like a baby."
>
> "No I don't, Aunty. I'm in Year One now."
>
> "Yes you do. You won't go to sleep with the light off."
>
> "Mum, will you come and stay with me while I go to sleep?"

As a parent, you start in a good position. You are interested in the development of your children; you are concerned about them and their future; you know and love them. Another quality that it is important for parents to possess is respect for their children. This means that youngsters have needs, concerns, and wants which they wish to express and have considered. Their needs are as important as anyone else's when it comes to making a decision, even if the final decision is not the one they would

Children's needs are as important as anyone else's

like. I am often surprised when people direct questions to me about what my children would like when they are present. They are capable of answering for themselves and will know just how they are feeling at that time.

> *"Would Pat like chips or mashed potatoes?"*
>
> *"I'm not sure. He likes them both. Why don't you ask him?"*

Remember that today will not last for long

Remember that today will not last for long. By tomorrow, your children may have changed as they move along the path of childhood. Enjoy your kids while you can. Become friends with them now so that you will have a firm foundation for your relationship in the future.

Our job as parents is not to force our children to behave as we wish but to encourage them to behave the way we want them to. It is as though you are a gardener and they are the flowers (the person who invented the term kindergarten was right — a garden of children). They each have a life force, and they are slightly different from one another, but they also have many similarities. It is up to you to encourage the blooms, to train the branches and to nourish the roots. If you can do this in a patient, generous, happy, and loving way, I'm sure you will be blessed with a bountiful garden.

1
THE AGES AND STAGES OF GROWTH

Each age has its own rewards, and its own difficulties

What is 'normal'?

Most parents are concerned about their child's development. They particularly worry about whether their child is "normal". To gauge this normality, some will compare their child to schoolfriends or cousins. This is not really satisfactory. How do they know that the child being used as a comparison is "normal"? Although there are fairly general indicators of what you can expect of your child at each age or stage during this period of development, there is a wide variation in what may be considered normal. These variations may appear as differences in height or weight, ability to read, spell, write, play sports and so on.

> *John is a five-year-old boy who has four adult teeth and has shed several other milk teeth. Belinda is a seven-year-old girl who has a perfect set of milk teeth; she has not shed any of them. Both of these children are normal, though perhaps a little faster and a little slower in development than children of their age.*

Comparing your child with another can be of little real help, since every child is different

Comparing your child with another, although a common thing for parents to do, can be of little real help, since every child is slightly different from everyone else. The rate of growth is not only controlled by age but also by heredity. A child with two short parents is less likely to grow into a tall adult than one with either or both parents taller than average.

Nutrition and health are among the factors involved in determining the eventual height, weight, or ability of a child. The growth of most children will even out over time. Some grow quickly in this part of their childhood and appear to stand out against their classmates, but most of the others will catch up in adolescence.

In comparison to infancy, which is a time of rapid development, growth during the five-to-eleven period is relatively slow. Children in this age group are likely to grow about six centimetres in height and put on about three and a half kilograms of weight per year. The weight gain is usually more muscle than fat, which explains why kids become stronger and faster throughout this period. In adolescence they will once again go through a period of rapid growth.

What then are the recognised changes that occur at different ages throughout this period of a child's life? As a parent, you may find it hard to identify the changes that occur in your children, until you look back to what tasks they could or couldn't do in the past. Sometimes looking at photographs will prompt you to realise how much they have actually changed even in a short period of time.

Another way of looking at the development of children is by *stages*. This has been popular with many psychologists, as it is less specific and allows for the variations that occur between children of the same age. However, not many of them agree on what these stages are or what they really mean. So, instead of discussing the details of these theories, I will mostly refer to Piaget's theory to explain the behaviour of children at different ages, since his is one of the most widely accepted theories.

Piaget suggests that until about seven years old children are *pre-operational*. They see things as being one of two possible dimensions, such as good/bad or right/wrong. They are also not able to correctly guess what will happen next or reverse a process back to the beginning. This type of thinking makes them have a fairly rigid view of the world and how it operates.

Children from about seven to eleven think at the *concrete operations* level. They are less rigid in their thinking than their younger friends. They can now think through a sequence of events as well as go through the steps back to the beginning. From about eleven years of age children move into the *formal operations* level of thinking, according to Piaget. This final level, which continues to adulthood, is characterised by logical, creative and abstract thinking.

The recognised changes of a child's life

Fabulous Five

Fives are wonderful little people. If you happen to meet a five-year-old and enter into a conversation, you will quickly be told that your new friend is five. This age is definitely a milestone in a child's development. Fives have come a long way in those few years. They have a sense of who they are, who they are related to, what they like and dislike, who their friends are, and what they enjoy doing.

Fives are wonderful little people

> "Hello, Elizabeth, how are you?"
>
> "Hi. How come you're here? Did you know I'm five now?"
>
> "Five! You're getting really old."
>
> "Yes, I'm in big school too."

Fives can feed themselves, although they still need someone to cut their food for them. Sandwiches are easy at school, as are small pieces of fruit. The only problem is that they can be very slow in finishing a meal, though they now like to finish it and are pleased with a "clean plate". A small serve may seem like a solution to the problem of slowness, but it probably will not work, as they also have good appetites. Their improved appetite is their body's way of coping with the extra demands that are being placed on it by school and other vigorous activities.

Although they can dress themselves and will happily do so if their clothes are accessible, they sometimes end up with their clothes on inside out or back-to-front. When choosing clothing for this age group, it is still advisable to get garments that pull on and have a minimum of buttons or zips at the back or buttons on the cuffs. Tracksuits, pull-on shorts, jeans, or skirts, T-shirts, and skivvies are ideal. There seems to be a move in many primary schools to go for such clothing in uniforms, especially in winter. Some five-year-olds can tie their shoelaces, but many still need help. Some may have difficulty in working out which shoe fits which foot.

> "Mum, I'm finished."
>
> "Have you washed your knees?"
>
> "Yes."
>
> "Your face and neck?"
>
> "Yes."
>
> "Your feet and fingers?"
>
> "Yes."
>
> "Okay, I'm bringing the towel."

Fives can also manage to bath themselves. It will be faster and more productive if a parent stays in range of the bathroom to suggest the next bit that needs washing; otherwise you may get two very clean knees and a dirty face emerging from the bathtub.

Five-year-olds are more able to use the toilet unaided. They usually recognise the message but sometimes may be too involved in what they are doing to go to the toilet, so there is a last-minute rush which may result in soiling. After using the toilet, they may also forget to use toilet paper, so it is a good idea to call out and remind them before they have finished.

It can be helpful if you drill them about how to care for themselves after using the toilet, because you will not be available at school to help them. Some schools arrange for the kinders to use the toilets before or after recess so that the teachers can help them and not have the bigger kids getting in their way. A spare pair of undies in the schoolbag may be helpful in case of accidents.

Fives may need to get up during the night to use the toilet. Having a potty and a nightlight in their room can save them from having to wander around the house in the dark or wake you up to help them.

With an increased vocabulary and improved ability at stringing words together, fives are great talkers. Sometimes they have difficulties in getting out what they want to say because they are in such a rush to tell you everything. It is better if you let them say what they want instead of trying to help by saying it for them. They can become frustrated and may start to stutter or decide to avoid talking to you because you make them feel uncomfortable.

Fives are great talkers

"Mum, we had a great day at school."

"What happened that was such fun?"

"Well, you know . . . umm . . . ahh . . . what's-his-name?"

"Simon?"

"No, you know . . . umm . . ."

"Brad?"

"Oh, I don't remember. I'm going to watch TV."

"But don't you want to tell me what happened today?"

"No. It doesn't really matter."

Fives like to play, especially with another child of the same age. They also like you to read to them. If given the chance they will appear to "read" a favourite story. They are also starting to write letters of the alphabet and usually begin with ones that relate to them, especially the letters of their name. It's best to check with their teacher about the kind of script they should be using so that you don't confuse them by using a different one at home to the one they are learning at school.

Once at school, fives adjust quite well, though some of them find it very tiring. They will cope better with school if they get plenty of sleep. Some may actually need a nap as soon as they come home from school. Others may need an early dinner and be in bed straight after so that they can get the eleven or so hours of sleep that they need to keep them going throughout the day.

Fives do not like to take the blame when things go wrong. They will blame anyone who is close by for the problem that has occurred. Basically it is of little use arguing with them. It is better if you try not to let such situations occur and realise that they will be able to accept the blame in the future when they have grown a little more.

> **Fives do not like to take the blame when things go wrong. They will blame anyone who is close by**

> "David, you are a bad boy for making a mess by spilling your drink."
>
> "It wasn't my fault."
>
> "Yes it was. I don't know why you are so bad?"
>
> "But I was only trying to pour myself a drink!"
>
> "Did you ask me to pour that for you?"
>
> "Yes, because I thought I might spill it, but you took too long."
>
> "I'm sorry. You're not a bad boy, just a bit clumsy sometimes."

The reason why you will not be able to change their mind is that fives are in the pre-operational stage of thinking referred to earlier. To them, everything is black or white, good or bad, there is nothing in between, no grey areas. If they do not believe that the accident was their fault, then it must have been yours.

This way of thinking has many implications about the way fives react to life in general. If you tell them that they are bad because of the way they have behaved, then they may believe that they are bad, not that their behaviour is bad. It is very important that you phrase your comments in such a way as to make them believe that they are good, even if they are behaving in a naughty way at the moment.

Fives may get into arguments with older brothers and sisters because of their rigid thinking. The older ones will be able to see other possibilities and will try to convince the five-year-olds that they are wrong. It is better to get them to agree to disagree and to explain to the older child that the younger brother or sister is not able to understand the difference yet and the older child should make allowances for this.

> *"Mum, Matthew's picking on me."*
>
> *"Matt, what's this about?"*
>
> *"She's stupid. I was just telling her what's right but she won't listen."*
>
> *"You know she doesn't understand those things yet so just leave her alone. You and I know what's right, so that's all that matters."*
>
> *"Okay, Mum, but I still think she's stupid."*

Kisses and cuddles

Fives can be very affectionate and like kisses and cuddles from both their parents. Sometimes, if they have a bad dream, they may want to hop into your bed for a reassuring cuddle. They also like to cuddle younger children and generally think that babies are wonderful. Although they may know that babies grow in their mother's tummies, they are not particularly interested in how they got there.

If they do ask about babies and where they come from, it is best to listen carefully to their question for a clue as to what they want to know about. Some parents launch into a detailed description of human anatomy when all the child really wanted to know was where did the people next door go to get their new baby. Answer each question as fully as you can without going beyond their ability to understand.

If you have not already done so, think about what terms you are going to use about genitalia, because talking about back bottoms, wee wee bottoms, willies and dongers can sound very silly after a few years. Even though someone could have invented more attractive terms than penis and vagina, they are just as acceptable to kids as any other words.

Fives can understand about manners, though they may not often appear to display them spontaneously. One way to help make their appearance more regular is to play a game about having a "manners box". The idea is that if you want them to behave better than usual, you can tell them to get their manners out of the "manners box". If they have behaved as desired, then you can tell them to put their manners away until they are needed again.

Enjoy your five-year-old, because fives soon move on towards six, when their behaviour changes dramatically.

Enjoy your five-year-old

Super Six

Six is a very active time of life. A six-year-old rushing along may leave a trail of wreckage behind. Clothing, toys, games and the like are taken up and abandoned very quickly.

This activity can also express itself in indecision. Sixes want to get going and do things but they are not sure what to choose. Having started one activity they will quickly jump to another.

Their indecision may produce extremes of behaviour, where they go from being very good to very bad, from saying that they love you to almost immediately saying that they hate you. It can be exasperating for a loving parent trying to keep up with them and please them.

Reducing the number of choices they have may eliminate some of these problems. It is also wise not to take their negative comments towards you too personally. Accept their protestations of love as genuine and comments about hating you as expressions of the frustrations of being six.

Sixes want to get going and do things but they are not sure what to choose

> "Mum, I really love you. Can I have a special treat?"
>
> "No, I've told you no more treats until the weekend."
>
> "But Mum, it's just a little one. Can't I have it?"
>
> "No. I've said not until the weekend."
>
> "I hate you. Everyone else's parents give them treats, but not my mum."

Any gathering of six-year-olds can sound rather nasty as they align and realign their friendships

Their explosive verbal attacks may be directed at their playmates and friends. Thus, any gathering of six-year-olds can sound rather nasty as they align and realign their friendships.

> "I hate you, Annie. You're not my friend any more. I'm going to play with Mary."
>
> "I don't want to play with you any more anyway. You're stupid!"

Their desire to be first or to win can also lead to verbal clashes as they argue with and bully their friends. This can be very embarrassing for parents who may be within earshot, but it is best to leave them alone. If you interfere and insist that they make up with their friend, their response will not be genuine. Nor will this give them a chance to cope with their own feelings.

Sixes tend to have good appetites, although this may not be obvious at breakfast time. If given the chance, they will often ask for more than they can eat or drink. Parents need to be aware of this and create some strategies to avoid confrontations, as six-year-olds are likely to dissolve into tears if their parents refuse to let them have what they want.

You can have a system of second helpings for those who finish their meals and provide only small plates and glasses for the kids, which if well filled make them think they are getting as much food as everyone else. Even this can create difficulties, as it is believed that children between three and seven years old are not able to understand that the amount in a short, wide glass is the same as that in a tall, narrow glass. They see a tall glass as being bigger and holding more than a short one. Thus, many mealtime squabbles can occur if children of these ages are given different shaped glasses. They will all want the tall one. Whoever gets the short one will believe that he or she is getting less than the others. A collection of Vegemite jars with pop-off lids may solve such difficulties. Everyone gets the same, and the containers only hold a child-sized amount. And if they are broken, it is no great loss.

> "I want two hamburgers, a large packet of chips and a big milkshake."
>
> "I think that might be too much for you to eat."
>
> "No, it won't. I'm really hungry."
>
> "How about having one hamburger and a small serve of chips to begin with. If you're still hungry after you finish that, I'll get you another lot."
>
> "Oh, but I'm starving."
>
> "But this way it will be fresh and hot."
>
> "All right, but can I have an ice-cream too?"
>
> "We'll see. You haven't started yet."

Sexist thinking

At this age, children tend to be rather sexist in their thinking. Part of the rigidity of pre-operational thinking is that they believe women wear dresses and work as nurses and men wear pants and are doctors. Some modern parents are horrified by such beliefs and wonder where they came from. There is no need to worry; when the children move into the next stage, their beliefs about proper dress and jobs for men and women will relax as they come to see the inconsistency of their earlier beliefs and what they see happening around them.

Sixes' continuous activity can wreck a family meal. Their legs are swinging, they knock things over on the table (quite often their overfull glass); they begin by attacking their food, sometimes talking with a full mouth, they find knives and forks a waste of time; and just as suddenly their interest falls off, and finishing the meal can be a very slow process. Sometimes it can quicken the process if you make it a race that they can win.

Sixes can wreck a family meal

"Belinda, finish your dinner."

"I'm not hungry any more."

"Just a few more mouthfuls?"

"Aw, I don't want any more to eat."

"I bet I can finish mine first. Ready, set, go!"

"I won! Better luck next time, Dad."

Sixes would probably prefer to eat in front of the television anyway. That way they eat their dinner and don't miss their favourite show. So if you are prepared to let them do so, you may be able to have a more civilised meal with the older members of the family at the table, only insisting on the six-year-old eating at the table for special occasions.

Many sixes still need about eleven hours sleep but may wake more often with nightmares or very disturbing dreams. They may also need a night light so that they do not worry if they wake up. Usually at bedtime they like their parents to read them stories and will be better at picking out the letters and short words that they recognise than when they were younger.

Sixes also like to discuss the day's events with you at this quiet time before sleep. Suddenly you will hear about all the questions you had when they came home from school. So it is advisable to set aside time for this as part of their nightly routine, otherwise you may miss out on hearing about it all.

Bathing is more of a difficulty for sixes than fives. They don't want to get in, but once there they don't want to get out. So be prepared; expect the battle, and be firm. Let them know the rules about bathing and insist that they have a bath as often as you suggest. If you give them a choice they will only become upset. Knowing in advance that they won't want to get out of the bath means that you can be in control, instead of feeling that you are being manipulated by a difficult child. You can suggest they hurry along so that you can read them their favourite book.

Clothes consciousness is also a feature of sixes. They are becoming aware of different styles and want to make their own choices. Unfortunately, they do not display the care for their clothes that such interest may suggest. It can be quite a task finding their "lost" shoes the next day.

Let them know the rules about bathing and insist that they have a bath as often as you suggest

"Dad, where are my shoes?"

"I don't know. Where did you take them off?"

"In my room."

"Are you sure? Have you looked?" Maybe they are in the bathroom. Have a look there."

"No, not there."

"Are they in the car?"

"Could be. I don't know where I put them after school."

"Have a look in your bag, they may be in there."

"Yeah, I've found them."

Basically, parents need to be aware of the contrary nature of sixes and see it as a sign of increasing maturity. While it may seem that they have reverted to the behaviour of a two-year-old, it is for a different reason. They are now aware of the consequences of one choice over another and would understandably prefer to have both. It is not that they are heading down the path of wilfulness; it is just that they are six.

The consequences of choice

Sensational Seven

Thinking about everything

In comparison to sixes, sevens are sensational. They are quieter, mostly because they spend a lot of time thinking about everything, mulling over their thoughts before they discuss them with you. They are also good listeners, because they want to know about everything.

Sevens are at a stage of increasing the depth and breadth of their relationships. Their teacher, from whom they seek approval, becomes a much more important person in their lives. They are becoming more sensitive to the feelings of others and will sometimes berate a younger sibling for misbehaving if they believe it is upsetting their parents.

> *"Stop crying, Jodie."*
>
> *"But I can't stop crying. I want the bigger glass."*
>
> *"You upset Mummy when you make all that noise. Can't you just stop?"*

Tantrums seem to be a problem of the past. Sevens are more likely to withdraw themselves from a troublesome situation, possibly with a slam of the door to indicate their displeasure, than to carry on about whatever is upsetting them. Their growing sense of right and wrong often brings on the lament "It's not fair."

Sevens tend to be less fussy eaters than sixes and are more able to eat with the kind of manners parents like their children to display. They may be difficult to get to the table, because they will usually be absorbed in whichever activity holds their interest at that time. It can be hard for parents to fit the family meal in around sports training, dance or music classes, and television favourites if they have several children to cope with.

It often appears that sevens are deaf, as their parents repeatedly call them or tell them to do something

It often appears that sevens are deaf, as their parents repeatedly call them or tell them to do something. Usually it is because of the high level of absorption in whatever they are doing. They may actually hear you but do not listen to what you are saying. It is best to get them to respond, so that you will know they have heard you, instead of assuming that they have heard simply because you called out loudly.

"Nigel, can you help set the table? . . . Nigel, come here, please . . . Nigel! Turn that TV off and come and set the table!"

"What, Mum?"

"Nigel, come here immediately!"

"Yeah, just a minute."

Sevens are more independent in their personal hygiene. They should now be able to use the toilet and bath unattended. Although they can dress themselves, they often get distracted in the process and end up half-dressed. When getting undressed, they may leave an untidy pile on the floor. If you ask them, they will put their clothes away, but you have to make sure that they heard the request. Girls become very interested in their hair and like to try out different styles but may need help with tying or plaiting it. Boys can usually comb their hair by now without assistance.

Sevens have a deepening understanding of being part of a family. While they enjoy this, they will often complain that they were adopted, especially when upset with their parents. They can also fight with their younger siblings and be jealous of what appears to be the privileges of being younger, such as staying at home during the day.

Sevens have a deepening understanding of being part of a family

> "Nobody around here likes me. You don't give me any time."
>
> "What makes you say that? We all love you."
>
> "No you don't. I think I'm adopted."
>
> "Let's look at some of your baby photos. You were such a nice baby."

Although still absorbed by many outdoor activities, sevens are becoming more interested in organised games, both indoors and out. Parents and older siblings or relatives can now play games like cards with them and not have to bend the rules to keep them happy. They start to join sporting clubs, as their ability to judge speed and distance is much improved. They are also good at riding bikes, though they may not be ready to venture out onto the road yet.

To sum up, while sevens may seem to spend much time deep in thought, it is all helping them to become more independent people, moving towards the next step in their lives.

Exuberant Eight

The eight-year-old is growing up both physically and emotionally. Eights want to understand the adult world better and will tag along listening to all that the adults talk about.

> *"Lisa, run along while I talk to Mrs Wilson."*
>
> *"But Mummy, I want to listen."*
>
> *"No darling, we'd prefer you to play with your friends while we talk."*
>
> *"Okay, but don't talk about me."*

They have a lot of energy and vitality. "I can't wait!" is the catch-cry of eights. Unlike sevens, who may be cautious, eight-year-olds are full of courage and daring. But they may not be aware of their own limits, and broken bones sometimes result!

They are also very hungry — they have to sustain this vitality somehow — and are better at using their utensils, so they can now cut most of their own food and eat in a civilised manner. They will turn bathtime into playtime as they fill the world with imaginary happenings. So be prepared for a watery bathroom.

Dressing is much easier, as they can cope with most of the buttons and zips unaided, though they may need help with those they cannot easily reach. They are very interested in clothes, wanting to choose those which they think are fashionable. They are more self-conscious, especially about appearing to be different. An unusual hair colour, glasses, extremes of height or weight are all features they are now concerned about.

Fortunately they become more aware of orderliness and like to tidy certain important areas. Most parents would hope this would include their room. However, if they share with a sibling it may only create a fight, with eights complaining that the mess is caused by the others. They will then try to use this disharmony as a way of getting their own room. They are very particular about their own possessions and do not like having others around who may not care for them.

Although eights can read well, they often like to be read to, especially those books they think are too difficult for them to read. It can be a good chance for parents to share stories that they enjoyed in their childhood. Classics like *Alice in Wonderland, Wind in the Willows*, and *The Magic Pudding* are entertaining for both adults and children. Longer books usually have fewer illustrations, so children can enjoy using their imagination to conjure up images to fit the text of the story. This can be a valuable as well as enjoyable experience, since so many images are created for them by television that they may lose their own creative ability.

Eights are developing a wider interest in the world, which is why they want to listen to the conversations of adults. They want to know about everything, and they are now more capable of understanding. You may feel haunted by eight-year-olds who will keep close so as not to miss out on anything. They will not be satisfied with half truths. They are now discovering things by trial and error. Having thought about something, they will present their theory to you to see if they are right. They are happy to look things up but may need some help as their spelling ability may be related to their understanding of how words sound, not how they appear; for example, *phantom* sounds like it starts with *f*, and *knife* with *n*.

Eight-year-olds like to collect things

They like to collect things, so expect your house to fill with cards, rocks, insects, leaves, or anything else which may appear worth having to eight-year-olds. They also like to collect money.

Money as a reward

Parents can now use money as a reward for doing, or an incentive to do, unpleasant tasks. Eights are also happy to put their money in the bank so that they can watch it accumulate while contemplating the things they will buy with it. If there is a special toy or game that your eight-year-old wants, you may be able to help in saving for it by giving the child some money for doing special jobs around the house.

Eights' questions about babies and where they come from are going to need more detailed answers than you have given them before. They will become more concerned with how the baby got into and out of the mother's tummy. If you have been honest with them in the past they will be able to accept more explicit explanations, though you should warn them not to talk about it with their friends or younger brothers and sisters, as they may not be able to understand it yet. If they lose interest in your explanation just leave it, and continue at another time when they show more interest.

Babies and where they come from

"Mum, Chris has a new baby brother."

"Wow, he must be really excited about that."

"Yeah, he was telling me all about it. But we weren't sure how the baby gets out."

"How do you think it gets out?"

"Well . . . through the belly button . . . ?"

"No. They mostly come out through the mother's vagina that slowly stretches so they can fit through."

"But how do they get in there in the first place?"

"The daddy has to put the seed inside the mummy to fertilise the egg."

"How does he do that?"

"When the mummy and daddy want to have a baby they make love. This usually starts with kissing and cuddling because that helps to make the daddy's penis hard so that it can fit into the vagina to leave the seed which is called sperm."

"What happens then?"

"Well, if the mummy has a ripe egg ready at that time, then the sperm will swim to meet it and make a new baby that will grow in the mummy's uterus for about nine months, until the baby is ready to be born."

Altogether, eight is a very exciting and enjoyable age.

Neat Nine

Nines tend to be more self-dependent than their younger friends. They are great talkers and like to try out their theories on others. They tend to perfect their skills, such as improving their ability in a sport, through practice with a great sense of purpose. They have a growing sense of justice and are fairer in their attribution of blame.

Group activities are of increased interest to nines. Boys and girls have usually separated by this age, and they prefer to stay in their small groups where they often discuss topics of importance to themselves. They are also likely to tease each other about having boyfriends or girlfriends, which can be a great source of embarrassment for them. One of their great fears is appearing silly in front of their friends — which can be caused by embarrassing things their parents might do.

> *"You love Justin, ha ha ha!"*
>
> *"No I don't, Zoe. Be quiet."*
>
> *"I'm going to tell him, ha ha ha!"*
>
> *"If you do, I'll never speak to you again."*

Fighting with younger siblings decreases

They tend to choose a group of special friends that they like to be with. If they have started up secret clubs or groups, the activities of these become more elaborate with secret passwords, hideouts and initiation ceremonies.

The fighting with younger siblings tends to decrease, as they are more in control of themselves and are not as jealous of them. They are more able to act in a responsible way and look after younger ones for short periods of time if necessary.

They have become much more pleasant to share meals with, as they are more aware of manners, although they may not always display them. They can eat unaided and are not in as much of a rush to bolt their food down as are the sevens and eights.

Bathing is an easier process. Nines quite enjoy a leisurely soak and don't see it as a punishment. It is another pleasant environment in which to contemplate life, using their increased analytical skills.

They are also easier to get to bed now that they can usually be allowed to stay up a little later (they need about ten hours sleep), and they are usually happy to read to themselves before falling asleep. They do not need to get up as much to use the toilet during the night, although they may be disturbed by nightmares. It is advisable to keep their reading and television viewing out of the "horror" class so as not to add to their nightmare material.

Nines are good at dressing themselves and can even manage some of the loose ends like cuffs and laces without help or scolding. However, unless reminded, they are likely to dump their schoolbag and clothes on the nearest chair when they come home in the afternoon. Having a system of rewards or fines will usually activate them to put their belongings in their proper place and encourage them to be tidy. In general, the discipline of nines is easier than in their younger days. Sometimes a few reminders are necessary to get them to do what you want; alternatively, the threat of losing privileges will have the desired effect.

"Katie, can you clean up this mess?"

"Do I have to? I want to watch this now."

"If you watch that now, you'll miss out on your favourite show tonight while you clean up then."

"Okay, I'll do it now."

Terrific Ten

You can almost see the adult being formed

Tens display greater individuality than their younger counterparts. You can almost see the adult being formed. They are more aware of the world on a larger scale and want to understand about what is happening. This growing knowledge of the world and increased understanding of themselves makes them more relaxed and quite pleasant to be around.

They can organise activities for themselves and thus no longer rely on you to do all the work for them.

> *"Dad, is it all right if I go skating with Paul?"*
>
> *"Have you spoken to his parents about it?"*
>
> *"Yeah, his mum will drop us off and pick us up in an hour, after she does the shopping."*
>
> *"Okay, sounds fine to me. Enjoy yourself, and be careful."*

After a decade of growth, they have finally achieved "double figures" and are justifiably proud of themselves. With improving memories, they are more inclined to find schoolwork more enjoyable and are even happy to do some homework.

Tens like their families and are happy to join in family occasions, but they also get along with groups of friends. Their love of the outdoors helps to use up lots of energy. Activities such as Cubs or Brownies allow them to be with groups of friends outdoors — a very happy combination for a ten-year-old.

Their love of the outdoors helps to use up lots of energy

Table manners are well within the ability range of tens, but they may choose not to display them except on special occasions. At least you know if you take them out or have friends around, they should be able to behave themselves.

Clothes are not particularly interesting to tens. Boys especially prefer comfortable old clothes to scratchy new ones. They become increasingly difficult to shop for, as they don't like to try the clothes on before you buy them.

As they can now dress, bath and feed themselves easily, any slips in these areas are either deliberately made to annoy you or simply laziness on their part. So encourage them to behave as you want and as you know they can. They do not value cleanliness, so many reminders may be necessary to get tens into the bath.

They will probably prefer to have a shower rather than a bath, since they believe it is more "grown-up" to have a shower. You may have to get the water temperature right for them and have a non-slip mat so that they can manage a shower without hurting themselves. Some of the girls may also become more interested in using powder, perfume, or bath salts to make themselves smell nice.

They also exhibit more modesty and may be embarrassed if nude in front of a parent of the opposite sex. So it is best to respect this awkwardness and, where possible, have mothers help the girls in the bath or shower and fathers help the boys.

Ten is a very happy age. Children at this age are more self-assured, more relaxed, and more intent on enjoying themselves than when they were younger. With their love of family and friends they are enjoyable to be with and pleasant to have around.

Children at this age are more self-assured, more relaxed, and more intent on enjoying themselves

Exciting Eleven

Eleven is another very important age. Elevens are on the threshold of adolescence. They are becoming more independent, more concerned about their future. They are at a point where they are starting to have an impact on their own lives, making decisions about what they want to do. It is necessary for parents to give plenty of time to their eleven-year-olds — time to talk about the things that concern them, so as to help smooth the transition into adolescence.

> *"I want to do really well at school so I can be a pilot."*
>
> *"What do you have to do to be a pilot?"*
>
> *"Well, I want to go to the Defence Force Academy in Canberra."*
>
> *"Gee, Stephen, I didn't even know there was one."*
>
> *"Yeah, it's only new, but I think it would be great."*

Most elevens will be in their final year of primary school. They will be having a taste of being the leaders, of giving example and direction to the younger children. It is important to encourage this sense of having arrived before they move on to the next step. When they get to high school, they will be the youngest, they will not feel comfortable in the surroundings, and will have to cope with the new demands that will be made on them. If they have felt confident and happy in their primary school, it will help them through this change to the more grown-up environment of the high school.

Elevens want to be independent, but at the same time they like to be part of a group, such as a sporting team. Try to see this as part of their development and encourage them to bring their friends home so that you get the chance to meet them.

Some may have reached the final stage of cognitive development which is known as "formal operations". That is when they will be able to think logically, foresee results, critically analyse the world in which they live and take responsibility for their decisions. Sometimes this critical analysis is directed at adults, especially their parents. So you can expect to have to defend yourself and your beliefs if you live with an eleven-year-old. You will find an eleven to be challenging but wanting you to set the limits.

You will find an eleven to be challenging but wanting you to set the limits

"Dad, can I ask Julie to go out?"

"I'm not sure. Have you spoken to her about it?"

"No, I thought I'd talk to you first."

"Do any of the other boys go out with girls?"

"I don't think so."

"Maybe some of the boys could ask a group of the girls to go skating or something. What do you think?"

"Yeah, that sounds all right. I'll ask my mates tomorrow."

Some elevens will be experiencing changes to their body. Girls may start to grow pubic hair, develop breasts and other fatty deposits, and menstruate. To be able to cope effectively with these changes, they will need your support, guidance, and encouragement. Discussing these changes before they occur will help to prepare them for their arrival so that they will not be overwhelmed or frightened. Let them know that it is normal for these changes to occur so that they can expect them and be ready for them.

Many parents tell girls about menstruation before it begins but do not tell the boys what happens to girls until much later, if at all. This lack of information can also be the cause of embarrassment, especially as most schools are co-ed.

To cope effectively with changes to their body, elevens will need your support, guidance and encouragement

"There must be something wrong with Joanne."

"Why do you say that?"

"Well, when we went swimming today it looked like she had a poo in her pants."

> "Did you ask her about it?"
>
> "No way! Don't be stupid."
>
> "It was probably a sanitary napkin. When the blood has been exposed to the air it goes dark brown."
>
> "Is that all it was. I thought she must have been sick."

Boys can also put on fatty deposits around the hips and breasts. Many find this embarrassing, as they have to cope with the unkind taunts of their "friends". They may also begin to have nocturnal emissions, or "wet dreams". It is important to let them know that this is perfectly normal and to put their pyjamas out to be washed without needing to make a fuss.

Talk with them rather than about them

Some children find such changes very distressing and they become embarrassed if they think everybody is talking about them. It is much more helpful if you talk with them rather than talk about them to others. Mothers can let their daughters know how they felt when it happened to them so that the girls will realise their fears and concerns are also natural and normal.

> "Mum, you know in that Madonna song 'Like a Virgin'. What's it mean?"
>
> "Do you want to know what a virgin is?"
>
> "Yeah, the kids at school laughed at me because I didn't know what it meant?"
>
> "Well, I suppose it's time to talk to you about a lot of things in more detail now."

If you feel unsure about how to discuss such topics, it is helpful to get books about the subject and make a point of going throught them together. It can be very confusing for children if they find their parents are too shy or embarrassed to discuss it with them. It leaves them with only the misinformation from behind the toilet block to guide them in this sensitive area. So prepare yourself well in advance so that you will be able to answer their questions honestly and directly. If both parents discuss it between themselves, they can both be involved in this process.

Eleven is a time of great achievement. Enjoy it with your child. Listen to your eleven-year-old; become a friend, so that as the turbulence of adolescence hits, you will be able to ride it out together.

Become a friend

Now that we have looked at the changes that do occur in children during these special years, it is hard to understand how some people can believe that nothing happens. Knowing about these changes, you will be more understanding of your children as they grow through these years, and you will know, too, that you should enjoy them today because tomorrow they may be different.

2
AND SO TO SCHOOL

You, the parent, will never again be seen as the fountain of knowledge that you were through their pre-school years

One explanation of why so little is written for parents about children in the five-to-eleven group is that they have been collectively given over to the care of schoolteachers. There is no doubt that school is a major influence on their lives and that it formalises the wider social influences to which they will be subjected. So let's look at school and what actually goes on there.

You, the parent, will never again be seen as the fountain of knowledge that you were through their pre-school years. They will be surprised if you understand what Miss Smith or Mr Jones told them, especially as you were born in the olden days.

They will be surprised if you understand what Miss Smith or Mr Jones told them, especially as you were born in the olden days

"Miss Smith said that there weren't any cars in the olden days. What did you do? How did you get around?"

"Well, when your grandparents were kids cars weren't very common. But my parents had one when I was a kid, since I was born long after cars were invented."

Schools are both effective and efficient in undertaking their assigned role. Effective because most children learn something, and some learn a lot; efficient because one teacher for twenty-five pupils is cheaper than one to one.

For this age group, the purpose of school is to socialise the children into the system (which has many similarities to the work system) and teach the skills of reading and writing. Writing is both the physical creation of the letters and putting those letters together to spell words. Reading also includes being able to read and manipulate numbers, which we generally refer to as maths.

The purpose of school is to socialise the children into the system and teach the skills of reading and writing

You might protest that you learned much more than that in primary school. This may be true, but if you had not learned to read or write, the rest would not have made much sense. Many different topics were presented as a way of making it interesting while improving your reading and writing and teaching you about the world you live in. If you did not learn to read or write at primary school, you had little chance of picking it up later.

Are They Ready for School?

Even for children who have spent years at child-care centres or pre-schools, going to "big school" is a significant change. It is common for parents of the almost five-year-old to wonder if the child is ready for such a step, especially if it is the first child. You usually learn a lot from the experience of starting your first child at school which will help you to make decisions about the others. The following list is a guide to the kinds of things children should be able to do before they start school:

- *Say their full name clearly*
- *Recognise their name both in written and spoken forms*
- *Know their address*
- *Use the toilet unaided*
- *Hop on one foot*
- *Hold a pencil correctly*
- *Cut with scissors*
- *Do up buttons*
- *Repeat a short nursery rhyme*
- *Count to ten*
- *Recognise basic shapes like square, circle, triangle*
- *Know about waiting their turn and sharing with others*
- *Be curious about their world*

An extra year at home — worth every minute

Although children born in the first half of the year are allowed to start school before they turn five, it may be advisable if your child is close to the borderline to wait until the next year before starting. That way your child will be the oldest in the class instead of being the youngest.

You may think your child will be able to repeat a class if the going is too hard, but this is a much harder process than you may realise. Not only are teachers loath to make pupils repeat a class, the children also worry about losing touch with their friends. They may also find it boring if they have the same teacher with all the same work sheets.

An extra year at home may seem like a long time to a pre-schooler, but if it gives your child a better start at school it could be worth every minute. Boys often find school harder to adjust

to than girls, and if they are a lot younger than their classmates it can be a burden from which they never recover. They may always achieve below their potential level, a problem that can be compounded as they progress through school. So, if you are worried about what to do with your child, it is best to err on the side of caution and allow time for the child to grow before starting school. There are no prizes for finishing youngest, so do not push your child unnecessarily.

Sometimes parents are more worried than their child is about starting school. It is better not to add to children's anxieties by telling them how much you will miss them. Instead you can emphasise how much fun they will have, and all the new friends that they will make, so that they will be looking forward to starting school. You can help them get used to school practices by packing their lunch in a box and making a special time to eat it. If they attend a pre-school, they will be getting a chance to practise such activities.

It is of benefit if they can have visited the school before classes start, so that they are familiar with the layout. Many schools offer an orientation day to the prospective kinder kids for this very reason. So if you are able to, it is advisable to go along so that you will both be comfortable in this new environment. It can be very distressing for a small child not to know where the toilet is located and have an accident trying to find it. Children may not feel able to ask a lot of questions in this unfamiliar environment, so the more they know about it the less forbidding it will be for them.

There are no prizes for finishing youngest, so do not push your child unnecessarily

The Teacher's Role

Primary school teachers are among the hardest workers in the education system. They have to keep thirty or so small children occupied, interested and learning for six hours a day! Any parent who has tried to keep their child happy at home without resorting to television knows just how hard that can be.

The teachers also have to supervise the playground before school, during breaks and at the end of the day. Somewhere along the line they have to prepare lessons, keep abreast of developments in education and get to know their pupils so that they can continuously challenge them to learn more.

Teachers can use all the help you can give them by establishing and maintaining good communication with them. If you have the time, I'm sure they would even be happy to have you in the classroom. Make sure you say hello to your child's teacher and offer any help you can. It will also give the teacher the chance to talk to you about your child in an informal way without the stress of report time — which makes you partners in your child's education, not adversaries.

Teachers can use all the help you can give them by establishing and maintaining good communication with them

"But schools are so different now!"

School may appear to have changed from when you were in kindergarten, but many of the important things are really the same. One big difference is that of learning for meaning rather than learning by rote. Instead of forcing the children to learn pages of seemingly useless facts parrot fashion, the teachers try to create an interest in the children and give them the necessary skills to investigate this interest for themselves. That way they learn by experience.

For example, if measurement was the skill being taught, then they would learn about what measurement is and how it can be undertaken. Part of the learning may be to measure certain objects. They may discover that the dining table is twenty hands long and that their hand is seven centimetres wide, thus the table is 140 centimetres long. No doubt more meaningful than how many yards in a rod, pole or perch.

Another development in education that worries parents is the practice of encouraging children to write stories even if their spelling is wrong. The idea is that if they get used to expressing

themselves in a written form first, they can be taught the spelling — or at least how to look things up in a dictionary — later. But if they are afraid of writing things down for fear of being wrong, they will not learn to express themselves on paper, and they will not learn to spell either, because the words will have no meaning for them. This has some parents worried that their children will never learn to spell properly. However, the children do have a chance to correct their own work and to check the spelling of any word they are unsure of, and then the teacher reads through their stories and points out any errors to them.

This is a much more demanding job for the teacher than standing out in front of the class pointing to the letters on the board as the children repeat them aloud. Not many people make their job more difficult if it is not for a good reason. Teachers do so because they believe that this method is better than those methods used in the past. So help them to use this method by encouraging your children to write stories when they are at home and help them see their mistakes. But don't complain that it is the teacher's fault if they do not appear to be good spellers.

If they are afraid of expressing themselves for fear of being wrong, they will not learn to express themselves on paper, and they will not learn to spell either

"It's all Greek to me"

Imagine if you were to learn Chinese. The teacher would teach you a few of the more common characters to begin with. Then you would probably move on to ones that were of interest for you, which may depend on your reason for learning a new language; if it was so that you could get about on a holiday, the kinds of phrases you would need to know would be different from those you would need if you were trying to translate technical journals. It is the same with teaching children how to read the language they can already speak very well. They have to see that it is worth while learning to read, that they will be more independent in their learning when they can read.

Also, if you were then trying to read Chinese to the teacher, you would look for the characters you recognised and try to fill in the gaps by your understanding of the story or passage you are reading. If there were illustrations, it would help to make this process easier. Over time, the more often you saw a particular character the better you would be at knowing what it meant. It is the same for children learning to read their own language; they look for the words they know and guess some of others from the illustrations.

Your kids learned to speak by copying you. Sometimes they made mistakes but in the course of time they learned that *cordigal* is really *cordial* whether or not you corrected them. They learned by listening to you and all the other people who spoke to them. If they had not been spoken to, they would have made sounds that might have meaning to them but not to others. And just as they need people speaking to them to learn to speak, so too do they need to be immersed in the written word to learn to read. Books and words should be everywhere.

Books and words should be everywhere

Have a look in your child's classroom. You will probably find there are lots of signs and posters, often relating to the children and what they are doing. This is so that they get used to seeing familiar words written down and get used to the conventions of our language, such as reading from left to right and from the top of the page to the bottom and beginning sentences and proper nouns with capital letters. Such conventions are not obvious from the spoken language and are only noticed and understood when children are given the chance to see examples all around them.

You can help by pointing out other words that are in their environment. You may not like billboards, but they often contain interesting images together with words. So a game to pass time in the car is to read such signs aloud. It also can give you the chance to discuss the anomalies in the language, such as how words can sound the same but look different — for example, *to, too,* and *two.*

Label objects

Another way you can encourage your children's ability to read is to label things around the house. The children will then become used to seeing what the names of objects look like when

42

written down. But if you don't want the whole house covered in words, it may be best to limit the labelling to the children's rooms.

"Homework? What's it for?"

Personally, I hate homework and believe that it is unnecessary for children in the infants section of school. However, many parents see homework as the only way they can know what their child is learning about at school. Teachers use homework either to reinforce lessons learned during the day, the idea being that practice aids learning, or as punishment for disruptive children, as they may not be sure if a disruptive child has picked up the information given during the class.

If you are not sure what or how your child is learning, drop in to the school sometime or offer to help out in any spare time you have. Otherwise, encourage the P & C to run classes for the parents about the new methods of teaching so that you will understand what is going on and be able to help your child instead of causing confusion by using methods that were current when you were at school, but are not used any more.

New Approaches

One of the new homework methods is to give a contract to the children each week outlining all the homework that they have to complete during the week, so that they can adjust their daily homework schedule to fit in with the other demands on their time. Instead of parents having a nightly battle to find out what homework has to be completed and forcing the child to do it before the next class, they are aware of the total requirement

Homework: when to do it

and can help the child fit it in with their other activities. This method is more suitable to those in Year 3 or higher.

A question that arises with homework is when the child should do it. Some parents think children should come straight home from school and do their homework so what they have been taught is fresh in their memory. Others prefer to wait until after the bath or dinner is over. I think that if children have to do homework, they should do it when it suits them best. Some children need a break after school before they can face homework; others like to get it out of the way so that they can relax and enjoy their other interests. Think about whether you like to get home and start work immediately or have a bit of a break first. Give your child the courtesy of making such a decision as well. The break may be as important a part of the process as doing the homework. In any case, try not to turn homework into a battle but make it just another part of the daily routine.

Tests, Exams and Reports

Assessing and gauging the performance of children is continuously undertaken by teachers

Assessing and gauging the performance of children is a process that is being continuously undertaken by teachers. This is done for two main purposes: firstly, it can be to check if the children understand the work that is being done in the classroom; secondly, to rank each child's performance against that of the other children in the class. The reports you receive may contain information about either or both of these assessment methods. Let me explain in more detail.

The first type of assessment is known as *criterion referencing*. This simply means that the children are assessed to see if they can achieve a specified level of performance. For example, do they know how to add single-digit figures — $1+1=2$, $2+1=3$, and so on. If they can perform this task, then they may be ready to move on to adding double-digit figures. If they are having difficulty at this level, then the teacher can undertake extra lessons to improve their ability before they move to the next level.

The second type of assessment is called *norm referencing*. With this, there is a standard set for the group and your child is ranked against others in regard to that norm. For example, the class may have a test with twenty single-digit additions. The child who gets them all correct is ranked as first and so on down to the child who gets the least number right, who is ranked last.

Those who get more than 50 per cent right may be said to have passed; those who get less, to have failed.

So when you receive a report, you have to know which method has been used to assess your child. Some schools use letters to indicate competence. For instance, an 'A' will mean that the child has performed very well and is in the top group in the class, a 'B' pass may indicate the child is doing good work, a 'C' could mean work at a satisfactory level, and a 'D' that work is less than satisfactory. You should expect to get some kind of explanation about such notation and what it means for your child in each subject.

Many schools make provision for parents to talk to their children's teachers about their reports. This is an important opportunity for communication which should not be missed. It allows you to discuss any worries you have about your children and their school work. The teachers also benefit, as it gives them a chance to see things from your point of view or find out why you think your children are having difficulties. If your children are doing well, you may like to know if there is more you could be doing to encourage their interest and abilities. Teachers are usually happy to give you some ideas.

Parents' Involvement at School

Once your children are at school, you will be invited to join the parents' association. These associations vary both in their role and in their title. A mothers' club may not be designed to exclude fathers but simply be a remnant from the days when mothers did not work and there was a job for everybody. So find out what parent groups there are at your children's school, and go along to at least one meeting. That way you will have an idea about whether or not you want to get involved and you will find out if they are concerned about the issues that concern you. You do not usually have to join the executive to attend meetings and let them know how you see things at the school.

Such groups can be of great help to the teachers not only in raising funds to buy extra equipment for the school but also as a forum for opinions about what should be taught and how it should be done. The current concern about AIDS and its effect on our society is a case in point. Some parents of primary-school-aged children may say they are too young to need teaching about AIDS. But that may simply be a way of avoiding the

Groups can be of great help to the teachers as a forum for opinions about what should be taught and how it should be done

Although children should be protected from the harsher realities of life, it is best that they be told the truth in a digestible fashion before imaginations run wild

issue. I know of seven-year-olds who have suggested their family undertake blood tests as a reaction to the advertising campaign aimed at increasing community awareness about this disease. Although I think children should be protected from the harsher realities of life, if they are being told something it is best that they be told the truth in a digestible fashion before their imaginations run wild with rumours. Thus, the parents need to let the school know about their wishes in relation to such a topic and then they should work together to educate the children.

A primary-school-based AIDS education campaign may actually be aimed at the parents. It could be arranged to have a guest speaker come to the school to talk about this disease and dispel the untruths that have been spread. If this lecture were attended by both the staff and the parents, they would have a common body of information to work with; so that when questions arose, everyone would have sufficient understanding to be able to answer them. If the need for inclusion of material in the classroom became necessary, then once again they could get together to decide how this should be done and what material should be included.

Information on AIDS cannot be taught in isolation. It needs to be part of an overall human development program which covers the human body, reproduction, contraception, and sexuality, topics that may need to be addressed by teachers of elevens anyway, as some of the girls will reach the beginning of puberty while in primary school.

Other areas of concern to parent groups at the moment include the need for and use of computers in the classroom, the quality of education, size of classes, and equality of opportunity in education. So if you want to have some say in what happens in your children's school, try to go to some of the parents' meetings and let them know what you think.

Speak Up for Your Child

Parents also have to be their children's advocate. The needs of a particular child can easily be overlooked in a large class. Unless you tell the teachers about problems or changes that are happening in the lives of your children, they may misinterpret their behaviour.

One five-year-old started to become "babyish" in her behaviour a few months after starting school. At home it was a daily battle to get the child to school. At school she was withdrawn, sucking her thumb and clutching a doll. It was not until the teacher and parent talked that they realised her behaviour was a reaction to the changes of teacher that had occurred during the term. There had been one student teacher, three casuals, and finally a new permanent teacher, all within six weeks. No wonder she was insecure. But neither the parent nor the new teacher had realised how much change had occurred until they spoke to each other.

There can also be the danger that your children and their teachers do not get along. If you hear lots of complaints about the teachers, it may be worth while investigating. Teachers have a powerful influence on their charges. They can make children who are having difficulties believe in themselves, so that they can achieve, or they can label a child in such a way that the child never breaks free of the teacher's influence.

Teachers have a powerful influence

"Oh, so you are being lazy again, Sam!"

"No, Miss, I'm just a bit slow."

"Well, I suppose you'll get nowhere, slow Sam."

"I suppose so, Miss."

What a start for a six-year-old!

Primary-school children are not able to speak up for themselves. They need to have parents who believe in them and who will speak on their behalf.

Children spend more time in infants and primary school than they do in any other stage of education. It is important that they have every chance to learn and discover in a very positive environment. Help your kids to enjoy school and you will be helping them to enjoy life.

3
GIRLS VERSUS BOYS: WHAT'S SEX GOT TO DO WITH IT?

People imagine and thus expect girls and boys to be different. Well, yes, we know there are some basic differences, but does it go further? Are their abilities different throughout these ages of five to eleven? Let's look at the areas in which they are supposed to differ, to see if these differences really exist and why they occur.

There are contrary views about how we come to behave like men or women. Firstly, there is the view that we are born that way; thus the differences exhibited are there from conception. Another view is that we become the way we are through the treatment we receive, that it is the way people treat us that makes us behave one way or another. Others believe it is an interaction of these two factors — characteristics we are born with and the way we are treated — which leads us to behave in ways that are considered to be appropriate for men or women.

Unfortunately, those on either side of the "nature or nurture" debate do not look for alternative explanations. They spend their time either finding support for their view or discrediting the other. You may ask: does it matter, anyway? It would not if the differences between male and female were seen as being as valuable as each other. Currently in our society, it is still preferable to be male, or to do male things.

Nature or nurture?

Sex-Typical Behaviour

Some behaviour is seen as being *sex-typical*. This means it is typically displayed more by one sex than by the other. An example is playing with dolls: it is more typical for girls than boys to play with dolls. Those who support the view that such behaviour is in-built will say that girls *naturally* play with dolls and boys do not. Those who believe that children's behaviour is influenced by the way they are treated will say that girls play with dolls more than boys because girls are given dolls to play with and are encouraged to play with dolls; boys, on the other hand, are not usually given dolls to play with and are not encouraged to play with dolls — actually they are discouraged.

> "Here, Mary, come and play with your Barbies."
>
> "But I want to play with the Lego."
>
> "No, Patrick is using the Lego. You leave him alone and play with your dolls instead."

It becomes very hard to see where inborn differences end and environmental influences begin

Boys are encouraged to play with transportation toys, construction sets, and blocks much more than girls are. So it becomes very hard to see where inborn differences end and environmental influences begin. This is where the sex-stereotypes of the parents, their attitudes about what are appropriate activities or behaviours for boys or girls, can also have an effect on the children.

From birth, if not before, parents treat boys and girls in different ways. Studies have shown that parents saw boy babies as being stronger and brighter than otherwise similar girl babies, who were described as weak and delicate, only hours after being born. Imagine how much this kind of attitude would have influenced the children by the time they were five.

Between five and seven, children develop sex constancy. This means that they see men as males and women as females regardless of their hairstyle or type of dress. Before this they are influenced by peoples' outside appearance. With their rigid thinking, they would see a man with long hair as a woman and a woman with very short hair as a man.

"Mummy, why do you say Ernie isn't a girl?"

"Because he isn't, darling."

"But, he looks like a girl."

"Why do you say that?"

"Well, she's got really long hair."

"But boys can have really long hair if they like. Does he wear dresses?"

"No."

"Well, he is a boy."

"I don't wear many dresses. Will I grow up to be a boy?"

"No, Georgia, you won't."

Boys tend to act more aggressively than girls. This could be because it is more natural for boys to do so, or because it is considered to be okay for boys to behave that way whereas girls are told it is not ladylike to do so. Regardless of why such differences occur, they do exist. I must admit that as the mother of girls I am often surprised by the boisterous behaviour of boys. Rumbling, as it is called by my friends who are parents of boys, is where boys play in a physical, aggressive, and encountering way.

Boys tend to have more difficulty adjusting to school than girls. It would appear to be because girls are more likely to engage in the desired types of quiet, attentive behaviour than the boys, who want to be up and doing things. Teachers tend to talk more to the girls in a positive way, both because the girls seek it and because it fits their expectations. Boys, however, are probably reprimanded for aggressive behaviour more often than might actually be warranted. This could be because many teachers in infants and primary schools are women and are more comfortable with the quieter behaviour of girls.

> "Will you boys sit down and do your work?"
>
> "But he's got my pencil."
>
> "Dom, give him back his pencil and do your work . . . What's up now Con?"
>
> "The pencil's broken and he's got my sharpener."

However, teachers also tend to encourage boys more than girls to try out different behaviours. So boys will be praised for being quiet and attentive, while girls will be severely dealt with if they become noisy and physical in the classroom. Nevertheless, if the behaviour of the boy is seen as being "sissy", he will be given a harder time than a girl who is seen as a tomboy.

Fathers often worry that boys will have difficulty in being heterosexual if they undertake too many "sissy" activities when they are young. This may lead them to be even more stereotyped in the behaviour they encourage in their sons. However, it appears that the development of sexual attraction is distinct from the development of gender identity. So even boys who play football can become homosexual, whether or not they played with dolls or tea sets when they were little.

One of the outcomes of this encouragement of boys to play with construction sets and girls to play with dolls is that later on boys tend to be better at maths and spatial relationships, while girls tend to do better in verbal skill tests. So sex-typical toys

Later on boys tend to be better at maths and spatial relationships, while girls tend to do better in verbal skill tests

mean that each group develops different competencies and discrepancies in their abilities. It would seem better if both sexes were encouraged to undertake both forms of play so that they would be able to function well in both spheres.

Physical Differences

Beyond the obvious differences between girls and boys, there are other less noticeable ones. Boys tend to have a higher proportion of muscle to fat than girls do, and this increases with age; boys become more muscly and girls develop fatty padding. Boys also have longer legs, larger hearts, and a more efficient circulatory system. While these physical differences may combine to help them compete more effectively against girls, there are other forces that also influence such interaction.

Competitiveness

Video recordings of mixed-sex competitions have shown that the girls are less competitive than the boys. Even girls playing volleyball who have shown in competition with other girls that they have greater ability than the boys, lose when they compete against boys. It was found that the girls spent more time talking to each other and stood with their legs and arms crossed when playing against the boys — hardly a suitable stance for running and catching. The girls seemed to be unaware of this difference in their behaviour and blamed their loss on the boys cheating.

At five, boys are slightly taller and heavier than girls. However, this changes during middle childhood, as girls start their adolescent growth spurt earlier than boys, so that by eleven the girls are about two years ahead of the boys in physical maturity.

But this difference does not get expressed in favour of the girls in physical ability. In the primary years, children's running speed increases by about thirty centimetres per second each year, but girls are usually ten centimetres per second slower than boys.

It appears that the major reason for the difference in ability is the amount of practice that each group gets. It is more common for boys to be encouraged to run, jump, kick, catch and throw; girls tend to sit and talk or play hopscotch and elastics. As a result, one area in which the girls excel is hopping. It would appear that we should encourage girls to be involved in outdoor activities more, so that they will develop their bodies as well as their tongues.

As peers become more important to primary-school-aged children, they tend to form into groups. However, the characteristics of these groups differ between girls and boys and over time. Fives are usually happier to play with one other person and do not show a noticeable preference for the sex of that 'friend'. By nine they will almost always play with same-sex friends and usually in a small group. Groups of two to six girls tend to play together, but boys usually create groups large enough to play their preferred game. So if they need eight in the team, eight will get together, if they need twelve, then they will find some extras.

Friends: yardsticks or emotional support

> "Hey, Nick, come and join our team?"
>
> "What are you playing?"
>
> "Just tip football."
>
> "Okay, sounds like fun. Whose team am I on?"
>
> "Johnny's the captain, and Tony, Tom and Bob are your team. The rest are my team."

These differences in the groups that girls and boys form are related to the types of needs that friends fulfil in their lives. For boys, they are seen as yardsticks for their performance or helpers in achieving a victory. Girls use their group of friends as emotional support. So they spend more of their time discussing topics of importance in their lives than the boys do with their friends.

The arrangement of these friendship groups also differs between the sexes. The boys have more loose, unstructured arrangements, so that extras can be added to make up the team, as long as they are not seen as being part of the opposing team. The girls are more particular about those who are part of their group, and much of the time they spend interacting is occupied with discussing who is and who is not allowed to be a member of the group.

The differences between girls and boys in these primary years are not great, but they can be used to separate and segregate children so that the differences become exaggerated. Until we can treat children equally, and value the contribution of all people regardless of their sex, there will be those who prefer to increase rather than minimise these differences. It will be better for our children if they all get the chance and the choice to develop their potential abilities to the fullest despite their gender, as everyone has something unique to offer.

4
SPARE THE ROD AND SPOIL THE CHILD?

Discipline includes rewarding kids for the right kind of behaviour and punishing them for the wrong kind

Discipline is an area of child management that is hard to achieve happily. Half the time you feel like Attila the Hun, the other half as though you are under siege by Attila. What, then, is the happy medium? How can you encourage your children to do what you want them to without stifling them?

Discipline includes rewarding kids for the right kind of behaviour and punishing them for the wrong kind. When trying to decide what to do, we often fall back on the methods that were used in our childhood, with the rationalisation that they can't have been too bad or we wouldn't be the people we are. However, if discipline in your childhood consisted of father ruling with an iron fist, possibly wielding a large strap, it may not be such a good idea to fall back on old methods. These days, with more concern about child abuse, it does seem distasteful to suggest that physical chastisement is the best or only method of punishment.

In many areas of our society, people are becoming concerned about the rights of the individual, children included. We have come to expect democracy in society and try to practise it in the home. This may mean that as children grow we allow them to be involved in selecting their own rewards and punishments.

It is also worth noting that it is important for the punishment and the rewards to be given when the critical incident occurs. So it is not wise to tell a child who has misbehaved, "Daddy will

punish you when he gets home", because the child won't see the punishment as being related to the bad behaviour and will also come to view father as some kind of "meany" who only comes home to dole out punishment — surely not the way most fathers would like to be seen. It won't make much sense, either, if you lavish children with rewards three weeks after they have been well behaved. A big problem, then, for parents can be thinking of the appropriate reward or punishment at the right time.

If you are angry about the way your children have behaved, you may not be able to think of a suitable punishment and feel like resorting to smacking as a way of expressing your anger. Asking them what you can do to teach them that their behaviour is not acceptable will give you time to think and will help them to realise the causal relationship between wrongdoing and punishment.

"What, then, can I do?"

At some stage you will have to decide what to do with regard to discipline. You will probably first have to decide which method you prefer using, rewards or punishments — or a combination of both. At the same time, you have to be careful not to create a "cargo cult" in your own home, where a child expects rewards for simply not misbehaving.

> "Mu-u-um, can I have a treat?"
>
> "What do you want a treat for?"
>
> "Well, I've been really good today and haven't messed up my room."
>
> "But that doesn't deserve a treat."
>
> "Okay then, if you won't give me a treat I'll mess it up!"

It is better not to make idle threats such as, "Stop that noise or I'll smack you", as you will be undermining your own authority if they do not stop and you do not smack them. If you are not prepared to carry out a threat, don't make it. Some older children may push you just to see if you mean what you say, which could end up with you looking very foolish.

Rewarding desired behaviour is better than punishing misbehaviour

Rewarding desired behaviour is better than punishing misbehaviour because it becomes increasingly difficult to find suitable and effective punishments without alienating your children. Often the problem is worse with adolescents, for whom many parents cannot find effective methods of discipline. A smack on the bottom may have worked when they were two, but may not be appropriate for an eleven-year-old.

Consistency

The other important point that you have to remember is to be consistent. This means that you have to use the same reward or punishment for the same type of behaviour and that the child has to have some understanding of the grading of those rewards and punishments. If you are not consistent, then the child may get away with a particular behaviour one time and be severely punished for it the next. This type of inconsistency is hard for children to understand; they don't know what is expected of them.

It is also important that there should be consistency between the parents, which means that both of you have to discuss what methods you prefer to use and what levels of reward or punishment are appropriate for particular behaviours. If parents do not agree with each other about discipline, the children will know and try to use this inconsistency to their advantage. They will immediately run to the other parent if they think the "harder" one is punishing them and beg the more lenient parent to help.

If your child claims to have been treated unfairly by your partner, it is best to reserve judgement until you have had a chance to discuss it with your partner without interference from the child. Some brothers or sisters are happy when the others are getting into trouble, as it makes them appear better. So they will embellish a story if they think it will help them. Other times they will come to the defence of a sibling, in which case you end up with two or more upset children howling at you.

> *"Dad, Mummy made me stay in my room for hours just because I accidentally hit Stella."*
>
> *"It wasn't accidental, you meant to hit me. I hate you!"*
>
> *"I'll have a chat with Mummy and see what this is all about. Until then, leave each other alone."*

This problem of consistency can be much harder for parents who are separated. They may no longer be sure what is appropriate and what is not. You cannot always believe what children tell you. They can usually make the parent who is disciplining them feel that the other parent is fairer, or more reasonable, which adds to the difficulties and the guilt that the parent is suffering.

The eventual result of inconsistent discipline can be what is known as "learned helplessness", where children no longer believe they have any control over what happens to them. No matter how they behave they will be punished. However, if you are consistent, they know what to expect and can decide if they want that to happen to them. This also means that you have to tell them why you are rewarding or punishing them and why they are receiving the particular reward or punishment that you decide on.

This problem of consistency can be much harder for parents who are separated

What's Causing the Misbehaviour

The type of discipline imposed can also depend on the type of problem you are coping with. Disobedience may stem from the child being seven years old, an age when constant reminders

I had one distraught mum ask me what to do with a five-year-old who looked like he was about to be expelled from kindergarten for throwing stones at the school building. There was no simple answer. I would have to know when it happened, how he felt about school, his teacher, and his parents before I would be happy about making a response. But without that information, let's look at some possibilities.

If he was seeking attention from his parents or teacher then they would have to think about how they might be able to spend more time with him. They might also need to examine whether they had been avoiding him and why.

If he hated school and the only way he could express this was to throw stones, maybe he was too young to start school. He may not have been ready for the discipline and structure of school life.

If there were other things that had made him angry, then they too would have to be explored. He would need to be given the chance to explain himself, something he may find very difficult. So he would need to be given time and support so as to be able to express his difficulties. It could be that his parents were fighting and that this is worrying him.

Unfortunately, parents do not always have the opportunity to go through such a process. The child may be punished with a smack on the bottom and told not to misbehave in the future. He has now been punished in such a way that he probably feels resentful towards his punisher. This resentment will fester and grow unless he gets the chance to express his real difficulties.

Imagine how bad it can feel for a child if this process keeps occurring. Children keep bottling up their difficulties until one day they explode and they do something like setting fire to their school because no one has ever listened to them and tried to really help them. They have simply been punished for the way they have behaved. No one tried to understand why that behaviour was occurring.

are needed before any action results, or it may be because it is the only way the child can get any attention. If the bad behaviour is to get your attention, you may need to watch what happens in your household, notice if your child plays up only when you are busy with other things or when he or she is bored. When this pattern occurs, children may just want to let you know that they want more of your time to themselves. So don't let yourself get caught in that trap too often. Either make time to be actively involved with your children in their interests (or in sharing your interests with them) or else help them to find things that captivate their imagination.

If there really is a discipline problem, where a child's behaviour either in private or public is not acceptable, then there are other ways in which you might have to respond. When children are younger, you can usually pass off whining, crying or tantrums as the result of their being tired. This may still be the case with the over-fives, although it is less likely as they grow. If that isn't the cause, what is? Maybe they are upset by something.

It is important to respect the child. If you find yourself being angry all the time and always seem to be yelling and screaming at the children, then maybe it isn't that they have a discipline problem but that you are feeling upset with your life and taking it out on the children. If this is the case, write down all the things that are upsetting you and find some that are easy to solve. Once you have got them out of the way, you will probably start feeling better and will be able to tackle the more difficult problems as well as no longer needing to yell at the kids.

Minding Their Manners

Although the idea behind the use of manners is to make our social interactions more pleasant, it is not necessarily a pleasant process trying to teach manners to your child. First you have to understand what is reasonable to expect from children.

> *"How was the party?"*
>
> *"Great!"*
>
> *"Were the kids well behaved?"*
>
> *"They were kids. There was lots of running around and noise, but they seemed to be enjoying themselves."*

Bad behaviour: to get your attention?

Respect

It is not necessarily a pleasant process trying to teach manners to your child

61

The other thing to remember is that your children are learning all the time. The more often you remind them of how they should behave, the more quickly they will internalise this information and surprise you with their good behaviour.

> "Grandma, may I please have another biscuit?"
>
> "Yes dear, go right ahead."
>
> "Oh thank you. I really enjoy these biscuits. You're such a great cook."
>
> "I don't mind cooking for people who enjoy it."
>
> "I like your cooking so much, I think you can cook biscuits for me anytime you like."
>
> "After such praise, that won't be hard at all."

Repeating instructions over and over

The teaching of manners is really a process of repeating the same instructions over and over until the child not only knows them but can put them into action. However, try to be understanding of slips. If children were born with the culturally appropriate manners already built in, parents would not have much to do. Try to see the progress that is occurring in their ability and reward it, as well as encouraging improvement where it is necessary.

Pocket Money

Many parents are concerned about pocket money. There are various ways in which you can use pocket money. It can be for the children to buy themselves some treats from the tuckshop at school; it can be as a reward for keeping their room tidy or doing other tasks around the house, like setting the table for meals; or it can be used to teach them about money and how to develop a savings habit by putting it into their school bank account. The way in which you and your children use pocket money probably depends on their needs, your finances, and which of these purposes you see pocket money achieving.

Eights like money. They dream of riches and power even if they only have a few dollars in their moneybox or bank account. They also like to collect things, like football cards, so you can stop having daily fights about money for football cards if you negotiate a weekly amount of pocket money that they can spend as they wish.

Money tends to be limited in its ability to motivate. It may be best to give each child a specified amount of money each week for their own purposes, which they may save or spend. Then there should be some jobs that they are expected to do around the house as part of being a member of the family. Linking the two may only lead to fights over late payment or sloppy work. If children want extra money for a special purchase, there may be other jobs they can do on a one-off basis to earn the extra that they need.

Motivation by money is limited

Disciplining children in these primary-school years should be seen as part of a developmental process, teaching them the necessary skills to function in our society while encouraging their independence to the point that they become self-disciplining. If you are too restrictive, they will not become independent and may rebel against you. If you are too lenient, they will be shunned by others who may find them to be selfish and rude. Explaining your method and reason for discipline to your children, will help them to become self-disciplining.

5
"I'M BORED": FUN AND GAMES FOR EVERYONE

As children's skills and abilities develop, so does their capacity to become disenchanted with any particular activity. It can be quite a headache for parents trying to keep up with their interests, abilities and friends. The period from five to eleven is when most children start to develop some interests that stay with them for life. So let's look at the types of activities that appeal to children in this age group.

Play

Play can be regarded as the work of children. It is the way in which they learn from each other and the way they can experiment with the things that they are learning. Wise parents use play to develop their children's interests and abilities. Unfortunately, some parents regard play as a waste of time. They prefer to see their offspring involved in more academic pastimes, like reading. Reading is fine, but there is nothing wrong with play. It is the balance that matters. If they have time to play and time to learn formally, then they will develop in all spheres.

Play: the work of children

> *I know of one kindergarten teacher who on questioning from a parent had to admit that she did not have play as part of her program. It was no real surprise, then, that the child complained that school wasn't much fun. Surely a bit of fun makes all our lives more enjoyable.*

Toys

What the "other kids" have

Most kids have a reasonable toy collection by the time they get to school. Much of it will have been given to them without their requesting it. However, once they are at school and within the influence of their peers they produce a never-ending list of requests for toys, from the time-honoured ones like bikes, bats, and boards to the latest television-promoted gadget or fad. No matter which ones you buy and which you refuse, the "other kids" will always seem to be one step ahead in trendiness and cost.

It is hard to pick the toys that will last from those that will fade. Who would have guessed that Barbies would still be around, stronger than ever, after more than twenty years? (If you were bought one in your childhood, you may be able to recycle it for your own children.) I know of many parents who resisted the demand for a Cabbage Patch Doll several years ago, as its appeal seemed to be a lot of trumped-up hype. But as the years have passed and the appeal has lasted, the dolls have made their way into more and more homes.

Each month, and more so around Christmas time, a whole new series of "super heroes" march across our television screens. (At least they appear to march, until you get them home and discover that they are inanimate and thus not very interesting.) In some ways I am in favour of these toys, as they make playing with "dolls" more acceptable for boys, but on the other hand they appear to be actively promoting violence, which may be something you want to discourage.

When you are buying toys, especially those that have been requested (demanded) by your children, you may as well be philosophical about it. You are not the only parent who is forced to believe that your children's social relationships will be damaged if they don't have the latest, short-lived craze. When they quickly lose interest in these toys, you can comfort yourself with the thought that you were right, while trying to think up reasons for not buying the next batch of "wonder toys" that they now want.

In the long run it can be cheaper to get the toy they appear to want most than to try for either a cheap substitute or a more educational alternative. Kids tend to be very persistent and no amount of trying to buy them off with something else will work. So you end up with a cupboard full of cheap substitutes that were abandoned very quickly as well as the "real" toy that they wanted. It is also best not to anticipate their interests, because what appeals to you will often not rate a mention with a child unless the child's best friend already has one.

In the long run it can be cheaper to get the toy they appear to want most than to try for either a cheap substitute or a more educational alternative

Games

One of the pleasures of having children in this age group is that you can teach them the games that you enjoyed as a child and possibly still enjoy today. Playing cards have a perennial appeal. For the fives, "snap" and other types of matching games can be a lot of fun. It helps if the adults and older children pretend to be blind or very slow so that the younger ones feel that they can participate. Older children will enjoy poker and other games of skill if you help them out until they understand the important points to remember. If you are not interested in cards, you may find that your own parents would be happy to teach their grandchildren; they will probably enjoy many happy hours together.

As the reading and reasoning ability of children develops, they can play many board games. Such activities teach them about taking turns, making decisions, and, often in the earlier years, how to lose gracefully. Playing games can be popular on holidays when television is not available or when visiting grandparents, who may feel unsure about the interests of young children.

Books

Most children would have a few books by the time they are five. You are probably sick of reading their favourite story for the thousandth time. But as their reading ability blossoms at school, they will become interested in choosing their own books. Some companies make it very easy by selling the books through the schools, where they give an indication of their suitability for the different age groups.

Basically, the ratio of illustrations to words changes as the child grows and is better able to read and follow the story without the aid of pictures. For fives, reading is mostly looking at the illustrations and remembering the words that fit them. As they progress, they will only need the pictures to add interest to the story until the are ready for "chapter" books, where they use their imagination to create the images.

The way reading is taught these days is called *reading for meaning*. Children are encouraged to read a book because it is of interest to them, and when reading aloud to the teacher they are not pulled up when they substitute some words such as *likes* for *loves* or *hits* for *hurts* as long as it fits the context of the story. The supporters of this idea argue that it is better to pass over a few incorrect words that maintain the meaning of the story than to continuously interrupt with corrections. These interruptions can force the child to read in a mechanical way, saying each word correctly but not understanding the story.

The cost of buying all the books that interest a child is beyond most parents, so it is worth supporting the provision of a well-stocked library at your school and in your suburb. That way children get the chance to read lots of different books at minimal cost to you. I suggest you always include a book with your children's Christmas and birthday presents so that they also build up a personal library of favourite books at home.

Some children who find reading difficult may not be inclined to read books. It can be of great benefit to them if they are encouraged by having books readily available and by having you read to them. It may be easier for them to read comics, where there are plenty of illustrations to support the words. Reading is an important skill in our society, so any way you can encourage proficiency in your children without overwhelming them will be of benefit.

Include a book with your children's Christmas and birthday presents

Music

There are many ways children can develop an interest in music. They may simply enjoy listening to music, they may want to learn about different types of music, or they may wish to learn to play an instrument. No matter what their level of interest, musical appreciation can start early. By the time they are ready for school, most children will have at least been exposed to nursery rhymes and probably pop music, unless you don't have a television or a radio. With a bit of planning, it is not hard to widen their exposure to include classical, jazz, brass bands and so on. Watch out for announcements about free performances as part of celebrations, and take the kids along.

This may be easier to do in the larger cities, but often smaller towns have local orchestras that perform on special occasions. If live-music performances are unavailable, you may be able to buy some records or cassettes and make a game out of listening to them, by getting the children to play along with simple percussion instruments like shakers made out of rice and an empty tin.

Once children are able to read, they can be taught to read music also. Unless you want to own an instrument, it may be best not to rush into an expensive purchase until you know that the child likes and suits a certain instrument. Some schools have a collection of instruments which the children can borrow while trying out several. If you had always wanted to learn to play an instrument but did not have the chance, now may be a good time for you to learn together.

Musical appreciation can start early

> *Janet was a young mother of three who had wanted to play the guitar. She was a little reticent starting at thirty but persevered. Now she is in a band that plays at functions, and all her children are learning an instrument, including the flute and the violin. Music brings pleasure to all of them and is something they now share.*

Although you may prefer your children to learn the quieter instruments, there may well be a big future for those who make a lot of noise. Some rock groups have made a lot of money, probably much to the surprise of their parents. You may be able to convince your child that Reggie Dwight's mum only had to put up with piano practice, not an amplified electric guitar, but as Elton John he has made plenty of noise as well as a fortune.

At least if you give children the chance to develop an interest in music, it will bring them some pleasure, even though they may never appear to get beyond recorder practice (James Galway's parents may have thought that too). If you like the sound of the violin it may be worth looking for a teacher of the Suzuki or Yamaha methods, which are particularly aimed at children. Once again, parents are encouraged to learn along with the child so they know what the child should be doing and can help out when difficulties arise.

Clubs

If you would like your children to enjoy activities with other kids and possibly learn some useful skills, there are many clubs that they can join once they are at school. Scouts and Guides, or Cubs and Brownies for the younger ones, have been popular with kids for many years. Such clubs can be helpful for children who are not interested in sport but want to fill in their time actively. They usually encourage the children to develop proficiency in various skills, including cooking, and to be tidy, responsible and courteous. So if you do not seem to have the knack of creating these abilities in your children, you may be able to make it appear to be fun by getting them to join such a group.

Developing various skills

However, membership of such clubs by your child usually creates a demand for you to be involved also. So think about how much of your time you are prepared to give. Some parents seem to be able to run the Scout troop, the soccer team, and the swimming club with unending good humour. If you are inclined that way, pitch in and enjoy yourself. If not, give those who do as much support and encouragement as you can.

Most of these club activities last for only a few years. If the children do not get involved when young, they probably will not later in their lives. So see such involvement as part of the joy of their particular age, and encourage them to be involved if they want to be.

Pets

Pets seem to fit in here, since they can be considered an interest or activity depending on how actively involved the children become in their care. If the pets were around before your children were born, you probably consider them to be your responsibility. However, if the purchase of a pet was the result of the children's demands for one, you may expect that the children would see the care of the pet as their responsibility. This need not be the case, so parents should think about how much effort they are prepared to put into caring for the pets, especially after the initial interest has faded.

How to enjoy having pets

The level of involvement in the care of the pets also depends on the age of your children. Fives should be able to put some food in the pet's bowl if they know what kind, where it is kept, how much to give. If you train them early in these things, you should have little difficulty getting the pets fed. However, I know of some children who don't like the smell of the food preferred by their pets, so feeding them becomes a problem. If this is the case in your household you may be able to get dry food that does not smell as much, or you could cook your own, or else get the children simply to provide the water.

Grooming sometimes presents a problem, although the difficulties vary according to the animal in question. A five may have trouble grooming a fully grown horse but little trouble with a Maltese terrier. So try to match the task to the child's capabilities.

One of the other problems with pets is cleaning up after them. Now, even taking the dog for a walk does not solve the problem,

as you are supposed to get rid of the excrement and not leave it to foul the streets. There are units you can buy and install in the garden to turn faeces into fertiliser. So if you have a large animal, it may be worth investing in one of these.

If it is a birdcage that has to be cleaned, the children may be able to do it, at least under supervision. However, many a prized budgie has been lost to the sky when the cage door has been left open during feeding or cleaning the cage. It is advisable either to undertake such tasks in the laundry or to keep a close eye on what is happening so that a disaster does not occur.

Children can get a lot of enjoyment out of having a pet. There is the companionship, the interest in watching it grow, getting involved in breeding, or teaching it tricks. With a bit of forethought and encouragement, you should all be able to enjoy having pets around the house. A child that is afraid of animals of a particular type can learn to like them if given the chance of close contact with one.

With a bit of forethought and encouragement, you should all be able to enjoy having pets around the house

Crafts

As children in this school-aged group grow, so does their ability to undertake craft activities. These can vary from knitting to building model planes. Most crafts demand fine manipulation by fingers and good eyesight. Beyond resigning yourself to years of decorations being supplied by the kids at varying levels of competence, you may also be able to enjoy these activities by encouraging an interest in the ones you do or did enjoy yourself.

To see your child enjoying both the product and the process of such activities can bring untold pleasure. However, it is important to remember that children's first efforts may not be very good examples of their ability. But they will learn much by having a go. If you only concentrate on the end result, such as the Model T car replica, you will find that their interest drops off when they have trouble achieving a perfect result in the early stages. It is better to praise each improvement along the way so that they can see a development in their skill.

Bicycles

Learning to ride a bike can be a great achievement for a child. It can give children a sense of power and control that they may not have felt since they learned to walk. It is much easier now with the use of training wheels, since the child gets used to the feel of riding and the use of the brakes before having to concentrate on balance.

It is important, however, to remember that bike riding can be dangerous. A child can easily fall and be injured even when using training wheels. You should ensure that your child has a helmet to protect the head. Those who ride BMX bikes should have protective pads for the elbows and knees as well.

Many city roads are very dangerous places for bike-riding children, especially those under nine who are not able to judge speed and distance very well. Some major parks have children's bicycle tracks where they can get to enjoy bike riding without the worry of possible injury from other vehicles. If there is not one of these available in your area, it may be an idea to approach the local council about creating a safe area for children to ride.

Riding bikes on the road is really only suitable for the over-tens. Even then, before you let them out on their own, school them in the rules of the road. When you are driving around, talk to them about how other drivers are behaving and the dangers that they may create. No matter how hard you try, you will not be able to protect your child from every danger. However, you can try to warn them of the more common ones so that they have some chance of protecting themselves.

Dancing

Many children of this age really enjoy dancing. Although it is more common for girls than it is for boys to go to classes, such as ballet, it is becoming more acceptable for the boys to get involved. There are many forms of dancing available, from classical or jazz ballet to Irish, Scottish and morris dancing, as well as the folk dances of other cultures. Such folk dancing not only gives children lots of good exercise; it also passes along traditions which may otherwise be lost.

As they get towards eleven, children might also like to take up ballroom dancing. Although we do not get many opportunities to use such skills in everyday life, poise and grace in movement are always worth encouraging. If they wish to go in competitions, the children can also get a sense of achievement out of being able to improve their level of skill.

Other Activities

Children really enjoy a change of environment

There are many other activities that you and your children can take part in, from camping and bushwalking to horse riding or kite flying. You are probably only limited by your bank balance and your imagination. Often children really enjoy a change of environment. A weekend camping in the country can be a great learning experience, even if they only learn to be grateful for all the conveniences of modern city life. Country children having a spell in the city, on the other hand, may discover that there are disadvantages to city life, like pollution and noise, from which they are spared.

Some of the other activities that children enjoy are covered in the chapter on sport. Children benefit greatly from having the opportunity to experience different types of activities. If parents see the five-to-eleven period as a time to sample a wide variety of the interests and activities that are available, the children have so many things to occupy them they will not have the chance to become bored. Your relationship with your children will be improved, too, if you spend some time each week playing with them. It will probably do you some good, as well.

6
YOU'VE GOT TO HAVE FRIENDS

During these early school years, your children will become friends with many people. Some they will remain friends with for life, others will come and go before you get to know them. What, then, is the importance of friends to primary-school aged children and why?

Until a child starts school, a friend is usually just someone to play with. This could be a child met on a swing in a park or one known for a long time. Length of acquaintance is not the most important factor to pre-school children, but an ability to play happily is highly regarded. It is also usual for children over five to play with others of the same sex. This seems to be a natural process, although it may be assisted later by schools that put pupils into separate classes for girls and boys. As well, after children start school their interests and activities begin to differ markedly, so that they have even fewer reasons for playing together.

An ability to play happily is highly regarded

> *Theresa, aged five, said that a friend is somebody you like. Someone you want to play with. Sometimes they can even be nasty, but you make up.*

After they turn six, children are more aware of friendship as being something deeper. They look to a friend as being a source of support. They see their friend as being someone who does good things for them. The relationship exists in a self-centred way, with the emphasis being on what a friend does for the child in question. As they get older, their view of friends and what they expect of them changes. They become more aware of shared interests, they see friendship as being expressed in mutual support, and they look for compatible personalities to share their time with.

> *Shelley, aged eight, said that a friend is someone you care about that cares about you. You play together. They rely on you and when you get hurt you can lean on them, they care. They stick up for you when you get into trouble. They are special. If you didn't have a friend you wouldn't want to go to school. The world would be an awful place.*

Groups of Friends

It is common for clubs to be formed by eight-year-olds. They make up secret passwords and have special meeting places. Such activities remain popular until about twelve, when the need for this type of conformity changes. Girls form cliques which may take the form of a fan club or express some other shared interest. Boys tend to form groups that can become gangs for those more inclined to unruly behaviour.

So if you have a boy, don't see his involvement with a group of other boys as being unusual, but encourage him to link up with boys you like. One way to do this is to invite a group of his friends around to your place so that you can get to know the other kids in the group. Alternatively, encourage him to play sport with the children of your friends, so that you know where he is and who he is with.

Between nine and twelve, children come to see friendship as a two-way process, where you give to your friends as well as take support from them. This is the basis that most adults also work on, which is another indicator of the growing maturity of the elevens.

Friendship — a two-way process

> *Donald, aged eleven, says that a friend is a good person who helps you out. Friends are fun to play with. They are not boring; they are interesting. Friends help each other out if they are in trouble.*

Cross-aged Friendships

Friendship between children of different ages is not really encouraged in our society. We tend to segregate children strictly into age groups and expect them to have more in common with each other than with older or younger children. In other societies, childhood groupings tend to reflect the age composition of families, and children of all ages play together and form friendships. Our society's attitude seems to be the result of our concern that older children who want to play with

Friendship between children of different ages is not really encouraged in our society

younger ones are socially retarded, which has negative implications for their emotional and intellectual capacity as well. As for the younger ones, we are somehow afraid that they will learn about things that they are not capable of understanding; they might grow up too quickly.

This segregation works against siblings becoming friends. We might expect brothers and sisters to tolerate one another, but because of our attitude to the difference in their ages, we do not expect them to become friends. In any case, friendships are expected to be made outside the family. Such ideas about how children are supposed to behave both support and create sibling rivalry. We tend to see the children in a family as competing with one another, especially for the attention of their parents, instead of playing together in harmony.

Cross-aged friendships can have benefits for kids

Cross-aged friendships can, however, have benefits for kids. The older ones teach the younger ones the things they have learned. The younger ones come to admire the older ones and pass things on to other younger children in turn. Some pre-school child-care centres are run in this way: they encourage all the children to play together instead of separating them according to age. Some schools have composite classes and encourage cross-aged mixing, but this is not common, often because the parents of the older pupils are afraid their children will be held back by being in classes with the younger ones.

Making Friends

Most children best learn how to make friends by watching and being with other children

Making friends is not always as easy as it seems, especially once a child gets to school and starts to expect more of a friend than being just someone to play with. To make friends, the child has to be able to *be* a friend, to offer support to the other child, who needs to be someone with a compatible personality, and the two need to have some shared interests.

Some parents, not realising the importance of these factors, may try to push their child onto others. This will usually have the opposite effect and end up with the child being rejected. If you feel that your child has difficulty making friends, it would be better spending the time helping the child to develop some interests that could be shared with the others in the class rather than pushing the child onto other children and hoping they will get along.

One six-year-old, on starting at a new school, spent much of her time out of class tagging along with her eight-year-old sister, who did not want her there. It was not until she took her elastics along to school that she made friends of her own and was able to leave her older sister in peace.

Most children best learn how to make friends by watching and being with other children. If they behave in unacceptable ways, the other children will soon tell them. This will have more impact than spending hours telling your child how to be nice to others. Children teach one another many of the important skills of being an acceptable person. They teach one another rhymes, games and jokes, all of which can be important ways in which to pass on kids' culture.

One or More Close Friends

Having a best friend can be very special to a child, particularly for girls, who seem to enjoy having a particular confidante. Boys tend to be more comfortable in groups than with one friend; being seen as masculine by the group is more important than having the intimacy of a special friend. With more emphasis on equality and the expression of emotions, it may be that these types of friendship patterns will change. Then boys will get to enjoy the closeness of a special mate and girls will learn to interact more happily in groups.

Having a best friend can be very special

Since girls are more used to interacting with one or two close friends, they often find it hard to play in a large group. There can be a lot of nasty behaviour as they make and break these intensely cliquish liaisons. Such behaviour in childhood can make it harder for them to create a power base with other women in adulthood, when they vie with each other not only for female friends but also for the attention of males. Boys, on the other hand, with their tendency to mix in larger groups, can miss out on learning the art of intimacy, which may adversely affect their relationships in adulthood. They feel more comfortable in the anonymity of the group which may not prepare them for the intimacy of life as part of a couple.

Ending a Friendship

There will inevitably be conflict between children. This means that at some stage you will have to counsel your offspring about how best to resolve a conflict or end a friendship as may be the case. Generally it is best to leave the actual conflict resolution to the children themselves. If you try to help, beyond offering advice and sympathy, you will be seen as interfering and probably be a great source of embarrassment to your child.

The ending of a friendship can be a very painful experience. How acutely the pain is felt may depend on the reason for the break-up. If it is because the friend or your family is moving to a new area, suitable celebrations may help ease the transition. This may mean having farewell parties before leaving and then having welcome parties at the new place. If the move has only been a few suburbs away, it may not be too hard to organise; if it is a greater distance, letter writing and vacation visits may be more suitable ways of keeping in touch until the need for contact is not as great or new friends have filled the gap.

A friendship can also end because one child has outgrown the interests of the other, possibly also because someone else has been found to be a more suitable friend. It can be helpful, when it is your child who has been rejected, to explain that it is all right to feel hurt, sad or angry. Even though children may not believe you at the time, they will be reassured to some extent if you let them know that they will make other friends. Telling them about similar experiences that you have had may make it seem bearable.

It is all right to feel hurt, sad or angry

Arranging Visits

Children enjoy being with their friends and will often demand to spend time with them at inopportune moments. It is best to adopt a policy and let your children know about it. You may decide that you are happy to have friends stay on the weekend, but only if it is planned in advance and is with the agreement of all the parents. Otherwise you can be out doing the shopping and be pestered by your children to let them take home their friend whom you have just met in the cereal section of the supermarket. Children do not always remember the other things you have already organised. So if they know that such a request will not meet with approval, they may not react as badly as if they think misbehaviour will get them the desired result.

Children enjoy being with their friends and will often demand to spend time with them at inopportune moments

"Mum, can Jenny come and play with me?"

"Not today; we have other things planned."

"But just for a little while?"

"No. You know that if you want to have friends over on the weekend you have to arrange it during the week."

"Okay, then can we have her over next weekend?"

"Yes, if her mummy agrees."

"Gee, thanks, Mum."

Some parents, especially when there are several children in the family, will not encourage their children to bring their friends home or to go to their friends' houses to play. You have to choose what you believe is best for your children, remembering that having friends is important in their social development. If you believe that they spend enough time with their friends at school, then tell them so that they understand why you do not encourage their friends to visit. Otherwise they may think it is because you do not like their friends, which can cause something of a dilemma for children. They want you to love them and to like their friends, so if they know that you don't like their friends, they may not be sure what to do. They will not want to lose their friends, but neither will they want to lose your love.

You and Your Child's Friends

It may be best to keep to yourself what you think of your children's friends. You can gently encourage them to develop new friends without actually commenting on the ones you don't like. If you do make negative comments on their friends, it may only serve to strengthen the friendship. It is probably best to comment on the features that you like about the friends that meet your approval.

> *"Sam seems like a nice boy."*
>
> *"Yeah, he's okay."*
>
> *"He seems very friendly and well mannered."*
>
> *"Yeah, and he's good at handball too."*

Making friends is one of the functions of childhood. If children cannot make friends when first at school, they may remain friendless throughout their school years. It is a necessary part of becoming independent of their family that children seek out others with whom to play and spend their time. It can be of benefit to your children if you encourage them in this process instead of seeing it as an attack on the family.

7
GIVE YOUR KID A SPORTING CHANCE

Sport is great fun for most children. It teaches them many important life skills in an enjoyable way. These skills include team involvement, responsibility, leadership, health consciousness, and how it feels to win or lose. Unfortunately, some people see winning as the only reason for playing sport. It can get to the point where all the fun disappears and sport becomes a burden.

> "How was your game today, John?"
>
> "It was fine, Dad".
>
> "Well, did you win?"
>
> "We played really well."
>
> "But did you win?"

A chance to do well

Many children who are not clever at school may find a chance to do well in sport. It may be an area in which they can excel, and this can help them to develop a positive self-image so that they feel good about themselves.

What's Sport for, Anyway?

Let's think about why children enjoy sport. Have you ever looked at a playground full of children during their lunch break? It is full of *energy*; the children use their energy in many ways. You will see groups playing various games. All of these games have rules, and most of them involve lots of physical activity. Children enjoy chasings or tippies, where there is lots of running, rules about who does the chasing, what happens when you get caught, which areas are okay to be in and which are out of bounds. Hide and seek is similar, but with less running.

To a child, such playground games and sport are the same. There is usually lots of running around (unless it is swimming, where there may be more splashing around), there are rules to be followed, there are members of your team and the opposing team, and it's great *fun*.

Is Winning Necessary?

Since we live in a competitive society, many people believe that learning about competition is important. And they see sport as an area in which this can be done. However, various studies have shown that competition actually makes some people perform below their best, because excessive anxiety about losing or doing badly gets in the way. So if you put too much emphasis on winning, you could be causing your child unnecessary anxiety as well as reducing the child's performance.

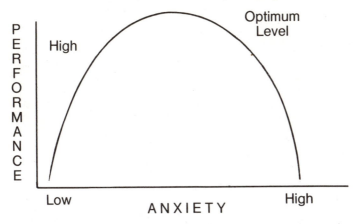

Excellence in children is important, as long as it doesn't get to the point where you are pushing them to fulfil your own needs. They may come to resent you if, by pushing them, you ruin their enjoyment. Surely this is not the result you would be looking for.

> "What do you mean, you're not playing?"
>
> "I'm sick of it. It's boring."
>
> "After all the money I've spent on equipment. You just get out there and do as you're told."
>
> "I hate it. I'm not going to play again, ever."

One of the hardest tasks for parents is to know the difference between encouraging and pushing

One of the hardest tasks for parents is to be able to know the difference between encouraging and pushing. All children can lose interest if they have had too much of something or if it doesn't challenge them any more. Sometimes the ear of a loving parent is all they need. Once they have expressed their concerns, they can then get on with the game. If you had pushed them, they might have become defensive and refused to play.

> "What do you mean, you're not going to play?"
>
> "I'm sick of it. It's boring."
>
> "What's boring about it?"
>
> "We've just played so many matches lately. We had the carnival last weekend, and we've been getting ready for the finals. I'm just tired of it, I don't get a chance to do anything else."
>
> "Sounds like you've had too much. But think of how bad you'd feel after the finals if you were not in the team."
>
> "Yeah, I s'pose so. Yeah, I'll play."

Everyone else is playing it. Why can't I?

Sometimes the pushing can be the other way round; the children pester the parents to let them play a sport. They can go on and on, whingeing and whining until you feel like the worst parent ever. You come to wonder if they are really going to miss out on something.

> "But everyone else is allowed to play. Their parents aren't silly like you."
>
> "I just think that you're too young yet. What's the hurry for?"
>
> "But all the other kids are doing it. You don't see them getting hurt or anything."

As a parent, you have to decide what you think is best for your children and stick to it. If they think they can wear you down by whingeing, they will continue until they do. If they know that you keep to your decisions, then they will give up earlier. It may be that you should look into their request so that they can accept it as a fair decision. Often talking to the parents of their friends will help you to make a really informed choice. Anyway, you can all present a united front against one sport and in favour of another if you actually know what the other parents think, since they are probably suffering the same from their children. With an increased concern in the community about the long-term dangers of some sports and the need for parental approval and possibly private insurance, it is important for parents to really think about which sports they will let their children play.

What Do You Expect?

Sometimes we can expect too much of the younger children in this group. Their ability to judge distance and speed is not usually very well developed until they are about eight years old, though it tends to improve steadily with age. Letting the littlies play in organised sports should simply be seen as a chance for them to become familiar with the rules.

Height and weight usually determine a child's power to throw, jump, run and the like during these years. Somehow, the children on the other team always seem to be bigger. No doubt yours will grow, but possibly at a slower rate.

Fortunately for very young children interested in joining sporting clubs, there are now a range of modified games available, in which the adult rules are adjusted to make the games more suitable for smaller children to play. In Mini and Mod League, for example, the length of play, the number of players in a team, and the structure of the scrum are all simplified to make it safer and more enjoyable for littlies. That way they are learning important skills and developing an interest in the game without being overwhelmed by the number of players on the field or injured through inexperience.

Fortunately for very young children interested in joining sporting clubs, there are now a range of modified games available

Do You Have a Gifted Child?

If you genuinely believe that your children are exceptionally gifted in sporting ability, then give them all the encouragement you can, although it is wise to consider the sacrifices that everyone in the family will have to make if they are to achieve national or international status. There will be training for hours every day, travel to and from training, and various levels of competition, much of which will be held at distant locations. And, of course, all of this will cost money. Make sure that you and your children really want to live with these sacrifices as well as the successes. If you all do, then go right ahead and enjoy it.

Which Sport to Choose?

Let's look at some of the more popular sports and the valuable skills that children can learn from them.

Swimming

Knowing how to swim is almost a must in Australia

Knowing how to swim is almost a must in Australia, especially with its mild climate and emphasis on water sports and seaside recreation. Local councils, swimming clubs or the Department of Sport and others offer swimming lessons for a minimal charge. So if you haven't done so already, do take advantage of this next summer.

The ability to swim can have many benefits. Most importantly, it reduces the danger of being near water. A tragic number of children drown each year; with a little more time, thought and effort, many of these deaths could be avoided. Swimming also may be one of the few sports available to some children, such as those that suffer from asthma. Unlike sports which may bring on an asthma attack, swimming is actually recommended as a way of helping children with this condition. As well, it is a sport where you can get fit without getting hot.

There are various skills to be learned in swimming: strokes such as butterfly and breaststroke, as well as freestyle, and also diving, turning, and pacing yourself. Swimming is usually seen as an individual sport, and children learn that improvements in their ability are a direct result of the effort they put into practising these skills. Improvements in breathing, strokes, diving, and turning all lead to faster times. The children soon discover that they are really only competing against themselves; their efforts are rewarded by being able to swim faster or further, whether or not they can beat anyone else. However, there are also team aspects to swimming, such as when the club or school is competing against others or the members form teams to compete in relay races.

Competing against themselves

Being able to swim allows children to be involved in other sports, such as surfing, sailing or water polo. They can also join groups like the Surf Life Saving Association, which accepts children of both ages from the age of five, where they get team involvement and can learn valuable skills such as first aid and rescue work.

For parents who have children of both sexes, choosing swimming as the family sport can make life easier, as they can all be members of the same club. That way you are not forced to choose which child you will watch or else try to be in two places at once.

Gymnastics

Gymnastics is a sport that helps children not only to develop physically but also to learn control and poise. For some children who have difficulty in learning to read or write, gymnastics is suggested as a way of improving their overall physical co-ordination, which is believed to have an impact on their reading ability. It can also be good for children who are afraid of contact sports.

Cricket

Cricket is another team sport where many different abilities are developed. Most of the skill areas require good eye-and-hand co-ordination. To bowl properly, children have to be able to position the ball accurately so as to outmanoeuvre their opponent. Batting well requires that they correctly judge the length and spin or swing of the ball to defend the stumps. Fielding, often the forgotten area of cricket, requires a good eye, strong hands, fast feet, and an ability to overcome boredom, so as to be ready when the ball comes the fielder's way.

The skill areas require good eye-and-hand co-ordination

Tennis

Tennis is another sport in which good eye-and-hand co-ordination is required. Speedy footwork around the court is also important so that the player can be in a position to cover the opponent's returns. Although young children may not have the power to hit blistering serves or returns, they can nevertheless play and enjoy the game while developing their strength and ability. Some very well-known players, such as Steffi Graf and Boris Becker, made world ranking at an early age, no doubt as a result of much practice during their primary-school years. The widespread acceptance of the two-handed backhand makes it easier for young players to play with their otherwise more competent adult opponents.

Football

The various football codes require skill in kicking, running, and ball handling

The various football codes — Rugby League, Rugby Union, Australian Rules, and soccer — require skill in kicking, running, and ball handling. The tackling and scrums which are part and parcel of Rugby football can be sources of injury and so have been modified in the new games designed for young children. Soccer is the code often preferred by parents who want their children to learn football but with a reduced risk of injury, at least until their bodies have developed to the point where they can withstand the pressure of tackling and scrums.

Football is also known as a contact sport, since players make body contact as an integral part of the game. Some children are frightened by this and may spend the whole season running up and down near the sideline to avoid the other players. If this is the case with your children, then maybe you should talk about it with them and possibly choose another sport which is not so frightening until they are older.

Netball

Netball — and its indoor equivalent, basketball — are team games which also teach ball handling, speed on court, and accuracy in throwing. Although these games have different rules, they have similar aims in terms of attack and defence. A modified game of *Netta* netball has been developed for under nines where the goal ring is closer to the ground and the length of play is reduced. Scores are not kept, as the idea of the game is for the children to enjoy themselves while learning the rules.

Sportsmanship

Sportsmanship: learned from experience

One of the qualities that children should develop from being involved in sport is sportsmanship, which includes accepting the decision of the umpire, knowing that losing is as much a part of the game as winning, and, above all, having a sense of fair play. However, sportsmanship usually does not come naturally; it has to be learned from experience. This is where parents can be helpful, by encouraging their children to be good sports. Let them know they do not have to fall over or pretend to be injured to cover up for not winning.

> "*Aw, that ref's crooked. He lets them get away with anything.*"
>
> "*What do you mean?*"
>
> "*Well, when we caught the ball he reckoned we were offside, but when they did the same thing he let 'em go!*"
>
> "*Maybe next time the decision will be in your favour. What about that last scrum?*"
>
> "*Aw, yeah, but he didn't see it.*"
>
> "*I think you're just looking for an excuse.*"

Badmouthing the umpire may simply be a way of diverting the blame of losing the match from themselves, something that children are very good at doing. It is best if parents show support for the umpires unless they have been really poor, in which case it is better to report the matter to officials during the game rather than make a lot of noise later.

Outbursts against the umpire, especially if made by your child, can be very embarrassing. Having a quiet word to the coach may be a way of stopping it. Or you could discuss it with your child when you get home.

> "*I didn't think it was fair the way you spoke about the ref after the game.*"
>
> "*What do you mean?*"
>
> "*Well, he was only trying to do the right thing. With all you kids and some of the parents yelling at him, it was very difficult. How would you like it if people spoke about you in that way?*"
>
> "*Yeah, maybe he wasn't so bad.*"
>
> "*I'd prefer to see you lose a match by accepting a poor decision than win by attacking the umpire.*"

Even though John McEnroe's on-court behaviour may sometimes appear to lack sportsmanship, it is important for children to learn that his behaviour is the exception rather that the nor-

mal way to behave. Greg Chappell's underarm-bowling decision was also widely regarded as a shameful way in which to secure a match. Such displays of poor sportsmanship may give you the opportunity to discuss the matter with your kids so as to encourage them to behave in a better way. I expect McEnroe's parents squirm every time they witness one of his outbursts, wishing that they had impressed upon him more acceptable codes of behaviour when he was a child.

Kids Code of Sporting Behaviour

☐ *Play for the fun of the game.*
☐ *Listen to the captain and the coach, and do as they say.*
☐ *Keep to the rules, and encourage others to do this also.*
☐ *Do not fight with the other kids in your team; they are on your side.*
☐ *The kids in the other team want to have fun too; do not set out to abuse or injure them.*
☐ *Do not argue with the umpire.*

To Coach or Not to Coach

At some point in your children's sporting career you will probably be asked to become an active member of the club or school's sports executive. Coaching, time-keeping, fund-raising and such tasks all have to be undertaken by someone. You might prefer to leave it to the other parents because you don't feel sure of what to do. But it may be important for your children to see you supporting them in this way. Nevertheless, only do what you are happy about. If you feel unable to train the team, you may find that there is some other job you can do.

Your children may also want you to take an interest in their achievements. If there is a special event coming up, try to make an extra effort to be there. It may mean a lot to your children to know that you care about them by attending such events.

It may be important for your children to see you supporting them in this way

> *"Did you see that, Dad?"*
>
> *"Yes, darling, you were terrific."*
>
> *"Thanks for coming, Dad. I wanted you to see how well I can play."*
>
> *"I'm really enjoying it too. Maybe I'll come more often."*
>
> *"Gee, that would be great."*

Another way that you may be able to show your interest in your children's sporting activities is to help them practise. As many sports require two or more players, it can be of enormous benefit to have someone else there to throw or catch the ball. Even though Don Bradman perfected much of his skill with the bat by hitting a golf ball against a water tank with a stump, he also enjoyed many hours when his mum helped by bowling for him.

The level of involvement in their children's sports varies between parents. I have undying admiration for those who are totally involved. They always seem to have the car loaded with kids and equipment. A weekend away usually is to attend a special carnival, and days off work are to help out at the school sports. If this is not your idea of fun, then don't get so involved;

Helping them practise

if it is, go right ahead. Although the children may not say it in words, I'm sure they will be really thankful.

However, some parents' idea of helping is to be sideline coaches during a match. This can be very distracting and confusing for the child. One coach is enough. Let the coach do the coaching and leave your children to do their best.

"Throw the ball, Annie! Throw the ball, Annie!"

Annie threw the ball . . . not at the ring but straight at her father on the sideline.

Parents' Code of Sporting Behaviour

- [ ] *Praise all good plays regardless of the team and the outcome of the game.*
- [ ] *Give the coach lots of support, and do not openly disagree with the coach in front of the children.*
- [ ] *Tell your kids to play by the rules; never encourage them to foul, abuse or attack another player.*
- [ ] *Do not punish your children for making mistakes. Encourage them to try harder next time.*
- [ ] *Do not force your children to play sport if they are not interested.*
- [ ] *Do not abuse the umpire. If you think the umpire is unsuitable, complain to the officials.*

A Sports Store in Your Own Backyard?

Most sports require some form of equipment if they are to be played correctly. Nevertheless, it may be wise to wait and see if your children are really interested in a particular sport before making any purchases. It is amazing how quickly kids become conscious of brand names. They always insist on having what their friends have, which is usually the most expensive.

Conscious of brand names

Six- or seven-year-olds may think that they are going to be able to play tennis like Pat Cash and expect to have the best racquet, shoes and outfit that money can buy. When they find that they can hardly lift the racquet, let alone hit the ball, the equipment may all end up abandoned under their bed. Meanwhile they have decided that they are now interested in cricket, since that is all the rage with their friends. Of course, they will expect another set of equipment to appear miraculously. Either encourage their interest in sports that require little special equipment or else borrow some from friends until you are sure a major purchase is called for.

Clubs

The social side of sports can also be very enjoyable. It can give your children a chance to have friends with whom they share a special interest away from school. Sometimes it is best, if they are trying a new sport, for them to go along with a friend. It can help to keep them going when their interest starts to flag.

Children also learn both the pleasures and responsibilities of club membership. They not only make new friends; on cold, wet, and windy mornings when they would prefer to stay in bed, they have to go out and play. They then learn that when you are part of a team you sometimes have to sacrifice your own interests for the good of the team.

Children learn both the pleasures and responsibilities of club membership

I have sometimes prayed for rain myself on a Saturday morning so that I could have a sleep in, but when I see that look of pleasure when they catch the ball, make the tackle, or score the goal, I know it was worth while being there after all.

Leadership

Sport gives children a chance to take on a leadership role, as captain of the team. Most children are flattered to be chosen as captain, until they realise that it is not always easy. Sometimes hard decisions have to be made which can really test friendships.

> "Can I be centre?"
>
> "No, I've chosen someone else."
>
> "Well, then, I'm not going to be your friend any more."
>
> "But I'm only trying to put the best person in each spot. Maybe you can have a go after half-time."

Behind a great captain, a supportive mum or dad

As leaders tend to be made, not born, in this age group, it will be a big help if behind a great captain is a supportive mum or dad. Let your child share with you the difficulties of the job.

> "Mum, it's not fair. I'm the captain, but nobody wants to do what I tell 'em to."
>
> "Do you give them a chance to tell you what they want to do?"
>
> "No, I thought I had to do it all."
>
> "Well, maybe everyone could sort it out together. Or else you could have an agreement about swapping around."
>
> "Yeah, that might work. I'll give it a go."

Sporting Disappointments

Injuries

Children occasionally get injured while playing sport, which can be a big problem for both your child and you. It will probably make you very cautious about letting your child play in the future. You have to weigh up the benefits against the dangers. You could suggest a change to a less dangerous sport. Otherwise, take out medical and other insurance to cover you.

Benefits, dangers, insurance

When put out of action by injury for a lengthy period of time, children will often be upset at missing out on being with their friends. Depending on the type of injury, they may be able to go along to the matches to show they're still interested.

No One Wants Them

Another disappointment for a child is to be simply not good enough to be chosen for the team. Coaches often try to give everyone a go, but some children are more clumsy than others and take longer to be able to play well. It is more likely to be the other children who will have little patience with the butter-fingers. Once again, helping out with practice may improve your child's performance; alternatively, look around for some other, more suitable sport.

Sports Heroes

Children will often develop an interest in a sport from watching it on television. In some ways it's hard to avoid sport on television but it can be a useful source of information, just the same. Contests such as the Olympic Games can show children a very wide variety of sports that they may never have considered.

I know a little girl who had a great interest in football and a particular team, even though she lived hundreds of miles away from them. Television actually taught her more about the game than she may have learnt at the sideline. With instant replays and minute dissection of each movement, she probably had as great a technical knowledge of the game as the coaches.

Such an interest can easily be shared by a parent or developed in a child who is not good at sport. Following the career of a well-known sporting personality may encourage the child to at least to have a go.

8
TELEVISION, VIDEOS, AND COMPUTERS

During the last thirty years, television has had an influence on our lives. Its impact is often unrecognised, unknown and hard to calculate. Most households have a television set, and our children tend to spend part of their time watching it. Modern parents may not have lived without television and may be uncritical in the acceptance of it in their lives. Yet it is a powerful influence on both individuals and the wider society. Let's consider the impact that it is having on children and see how parents can guide their children's television choices.

Television has three distinct purposes: to stimulate, to entertain and to inform. Since we are not told the purpose of the program that we are about to watch, we may find that it does not meet our needs. Those who dislike documentaries may do so not because the content is wrong but simply because they want to be entertained by television, not informed. Some programs manage to do both, providing information in an entertaining fashion. "Simon Townsend's Wonderworld" was one such program for children.

To stimulate, entertain and inform

A Five-Year-Old's View of Television

Remember, fives see the world in black and white (even watching a colour television), so shows that have very obvious goodies and baddies appeal to them. This kind of show helps to support their view of the world, but it may make it harder for them to make the transition to the next stage, since they have such overwhelming support for their view. Some will always see things as being black or white, right or wrong, and never understand that other conditions are possible.

Fives are more likely to retain information presented to them by television if it is given in short digestible portions, in an entertaining way. Since short unrelated items do not use the beginning, middle and end of programs to develop the plot, they suit five-year-olds. But the children like these shows to be presented in a familiar form, with identifiable characters. So "Play School", "Sesame Street", Fat Cat and Humphrey Bear all fit their expectations.

Fives are also limited in what they receive by way of information from television. They cannot think ahead to predict what is going to happen, but this means that they are also not sure when the show has actually finished. If you want them to go to bed and they do not have the advantage of an older brother or sister to tell them that a program has not finished, they will happily believe that it is over at the next advertisement.

Common experiences

Television can provide five-year-olds with common experiences so that they can play with others. They will know the features of regular characters on shows such as "Sesame Street", and will be able to play out the roles they have seen. Such mimicry can be a valuable way of expressing themselves and learning how to co-operate with others.

But this rigid view of the world can create difficulties for fives, as they may believe that some of the science fiction characters really exist. ALF, the Alien Life Form, is a curious mixture of a large dog and an arrogant teenager. You may know it is someone dressed up and that he does not really eat cats, but to a five-year-old he is very real. Young children may be afraid that Alf will actually eat Lucky, and have nightmares as a result. It can help them to differentiate between reality and fantasy if you watch their favourite programs with them and discuss what is happening.

Television and the Seven to Tens

The seven to tens have a more sophisticated understanding of television. They have some concept of the sequence of a plot, that it has a beginning, a middle and an end. If you ask them to tell you about a show, they will probably recall all the main points though possibly not in sequence. The actual order in which they recall the events will help you to know which are the most important features to them. They are usually not as aware of clever dialogue as adults are and often miss subtle nuances in the plot. This can be annoying for other members of the family, who do not want to miss the next bit while explaining what Alex just said to Mallory in "Family Ties".

Humour appeals

Humour appeals to children. They especially like humour that appears to break normal rules, like children playing tricks on adults. They also like cartoons in which animals take on human qualities and play tricks either on other animals or on humans.

Tens can also be empathic; in other words, they can put themselves in someone else's shoes. So when they are watching a television program they are able to imagine what it would be like to be that person. If you have a ten in your household, you may find your child very concerned about a favourite television character because the child "knows" how the character is feeling.

Fantasy Versus Reality

Unfortunately, some children become so engrossed in the action on the television screen that they cannot separate reality from fantasy. They are likely to try out some of the stunts that they have witnessed unaware of how objects on the screen have been contrived to appear real, such as plate glass windows being made out of toffee or some other harmlessly smashable material. For those over eleven who have reached the formal-operations stage of development in their thinking, the difference between fantasy and reality is obvious. They know that characters in a television series are only actors and actresses playing their various roles and that the program is not depicting the real lives of those people.

> *"When I grow up I want to marry Mike from "Neighbours". Then I'll live in Ramsay Street and be on TV."*
>
> *"Don't be stupid. They don't really live there, and he's probably married anyway."*
>
> *"But he's not married to Jane yet."*
>
> *"No, but in real life he might be married."*

However, one enduring fantasy that children have from watching television is to become a TV star. Many of them want to be a star like their favourite actor or actress. This would have two positive results for them: they would have the fun of playing the character in the show and they would be popular with other children because of this. Few understand the hours of rehearsals and effort that go into making a half-hour program. It would not appear quite so glamorous if they did.

Cartoons, Violence and Sex on Television

Some of the most popular children's shows on television are cartoons, and yet these are usually full of violence. Various studies have shown that young children do not see cartoons as being unreal but become very emotionally involved in them. The only way you can know that the children are actually picking up positive messages is to quiz them about a program as it progresses. To do this effectively really requires that you watch with them.

You may say, why not just ban cartoons? But cartoons are only part of a range of programs that present disturbing or confusing messages to children.

You may believe that because the baddies always lose and the goodies win, all is well. Violent scenes have been shown to increase the aggressive and violent behaviour of some children. After viewing programs depicting violence, they are more aggressive towards their brothers and sisters than similar children who have not seen such programs. Even adults' behaviour can be negatively influenced after watching violent scenes; they can be both more aggressive themselves or more tolerant of violence by other people.

Some seemingly innocent programs can give children very powerful messages, which they may be ill equipped to comprehend. One episode of a very popular Australian soap opera depicted teenagers using a motel for a sexual encounter. This lead a six-year-old to ask her mother if her parents had used motels before they were married. If the mother did not understand the context in which the question was asked, she could have given a confusing answer to her child which might have caused a lot of anxiety for the child. Such scenes also prompt questions from children about sexual behaviour, which creates a problem for the parent in trying to answer the question honestly within the understanding of the child.

Some seemingly innocent programs can give children very powerful messages, which they may be ill equipped to comprehend

What Can Be Done?

What, then, is a parent to do? How can you supervise your children's viewing so that it keeps within your standards? Basically, the answer is to watch programs with your children. It is easy to fall into the practice of letting the TV entertain the children while you get on with other jobs around the house or have a few quiet moments to yourself. If this is the case, then you cannot really know the messages that are coming across to your children.

Television is both a powerful positive force and a powerful negative force. So if you monitor your children's viewing, you can encourage them to watch programs that will be of benefit to them. This doesn't mean that they should have to sit through several hours of uplifting documentaries so that they can watch their favourite sit-com, but that with a little gentle persuasion from you, their understanding of the world can be deepened. By being involved in what they are watching, you can bring out particular incidents in the programs that are relevant to them.

Deepening their understanding

If, for example, the children happen to be interested in penguins at the moment and like to draw them and read stories about them, it would be a help if they could watch a show or hire a video about them. Then they can see what penguins are like in their natural habitat. Afterwards you could discuss the things you have learned while watching the program. Often such shows about the environment are shown on the weekend, when you may have the time to watch with them — much easier than organising an expedition to Antarctica.

Video Viewing

The advent of the video recorder has also influenced people's viewing habits. It allows us to watch one program while recording another for later viewing or to watch our favourite movie in the comfort of our lounge-room. This ability gives us more control over the content of the shows we choose to watch. So you can show your children the kinds of programs you want them to watch instead of having to accept whatever the television stations give you.

You can show your children the kinds of programs you want them to watch

However, there is another side to the use of video recorders which is worrying many people, especially those concerned with the upbringing of children — that is, the viewing of movies that depict explicit scenes of violence or sex — "video nasties" as they are commonly called. Parents who do not have video recorders may feel that this is of no concern to them. However, there is the chance that their children will be exposed to such scenes if they visit the homes of friends who have video

VIDEO NASTIES

recorders and whose parents leave such material within reach of their young children. If your children tell you that they have been watching shows that you do not like, such as these "nasties", ring the other parents who have allowed this to happen and question them about it. If you think that their attitude is too casual about such matters, then do not let your child go to their house in the future.

> "Do you want to watch a video?"
>
> "Yeah, we don't have a video recorder at home."
>
> "What do you want to watch?"
>
> "I don't know. Have you got any good movies?"
>
> "I think so. Dad told my uncle this was a great one the other day."
>
> "What's it called?"
>
> "The Slumber Party Massacre."
>
> "Sounds a bit funny, but let's have a look."

Kids and Computers

Many parents and teachers enthusiastically support the availability and use of computers in primary schools without really thinking about their applicability. For those who have had little direct experience with computers, they are regarded with a certain awe — and accorded magical powers far beyond their real capabilities. Many parents who are worried about the career prospects of their children see computers as being a key to success in the future. They hope that by having contact with computers their children will be better able to find a job.

Computers in the Classroom

What, then, is the reality of computers in the classroom? Children usually enjoy using computers, at least in their early encounters, especially if they are used for fun purposes like

playing games, which are not very different from the games in video arcades. (There may be some hope for those children who spend hours in such places, after all.) But there are other educational purposes for computers, such as teaching children a new language.

In the classroom, the computer can be a tireless and patient teacher. It will repeat an exercise over and over again, if it has been programmed that way, without getting tired or angry. It does not yell at children or give them harsh looks. So for subjects that can be learned by rote, or for undertaking recognition tasks, computers can be an invaluable aid to an overworked teacher. At this stage, however, it does not seem that they will take over from teachers, as there are many other teaching tasks that are just as important. Computers are really an adjunct to the more common classroom learning and can be of benefit to children who need extra work in language, spelling or maths.

Another advantage of having computers at the school is that it allows the children to become familiar with them and not be afraid of them; they learn to appreciate the capabilities and the limitations of computers. It is this type of familiarity that will be of advantage in the future. Not all children will become programmers or analysts, but in the many areas that computers are being used in the workforce, they will know how to operate them to input or retrieve the information that they need.

Having computers at school allows children to become familiar with them and not be afraid of them

Computer Games

Playing games and having fun with computers is not necessarily a waste of time. It gives children the chance to develop manual dexterity and improve their fine motor skills. So the kinds of games they play should have increasing levels of difficulty so as to continuously challenge their abilities, both mental and physical. Also, any introduction of computers into the classroom should be accompanied by lessons in keyboard skills. That way, all the children will know how to type, whether it be on an old-style typewriter or a computer keyboard.

Continuously challenge their abilities

> "Guess what we did at school today, Dad?"
>
> "I don't know, Kris. Tell me about it."
>
> "Well, we've got a new computer at our school, and Mr Thomson let Year Five use it today."
>
> "Wow, that sounds great. Did you get a turn?"
>
> "Only a little one. He says we all have to learn to type before we can use it properly."
>
> "Well, I'll bring the old typewriter home from work so you can practise."
>
> "Thanks, Dad, that'd be great."

Unfortunately, at this stage games are more readily available, and cheaper, than educational material. Whether this situation will improve with the increased use of computers in schools cannot be predicted. Some teachers are creating their own programs as a way of overcoming this deficiency, but it is a slow and complex task for which the rewards may be slight.

So while it may be useful to your children to be able to use a computer at school, don't think that they are being seriously disadvantaged if one is not available. Also, don't be alarmed if all the children talk about is how many they scored in a particular game. They may be getting worthwhile experience, as play is an important way for children to learn things. It may even lead them to develop a new type of game and earn their fortune with that in the future.

They may be getting worthwhile experience, as play is an important way for children to learn things

Which Computer to Buy

If you are thinking of buying a computer for the children to use at home, it is probably best to buy a fairly inexpensive model which you can attach to your television set. That way, if their interest does not last long, you will not be very much out of pocket. However, if you are prepared to take the risk, or want something more adaptable which you can use for other purposes, it may be best to check with the school so that you get one compatible with the school's computer. Then the school's software will suit your equipment and the children will find it easy to use.

Television, videos and computers all have their uses in our society. It is not that they are intrinsically good or bad, it is how we use them that matters. If we allow them to rule our lives, then we have lost something. But if we use them to enhance our lives, and the lives of our children, then we gain a lot from them.

9
HOW TO COPE WITH SOME OF LIFE'S LITTLE DIFFICULTIES

Some children seem to sail through life with few problems or difficulties. Others, however, do not have it so easy. For a variety of reasons they have difficulties along the way, which in turn present difficulties for their parents. It is surprising how many parents there are battling with common problems who feel very much alone. They think that theirs is the only child who suffers from such a problem, and they are often not sure of the services available to help them or how to find out about them. There are other parents who, having given their children to the education system, hope or assume, that, unless they hear otherwise, all is well with their child.

You are not alone

Let's look at some of the more common problems that normal children suffer from and the help that is available for them.

Bed-wetting

Technically known as enuresis, bed-wetting is both annoying and embarrassing to children. They may have bladder control during the day but once asleep lose it. They become annoyed with themselves for behaving like a baby, and embarrassed if asked to sleep at a friend's house both for what they are likely to do and for what their friend will think of them. So it is easy to see the difficulties such a problem presents to a child.

The parents also have to cope with the problem. They either sleep on the edge of their bed, hoping to catch the child before the bed-wetting occurs, or else spend hours washing, drying and airing bedding. They worry about their child's reaction to the problem and how to cope with overnight stays away from home.

Why Do Children Wet the Bed?

There are several reasons for bed-wetting, which is classified into two different types. Firstly, there is primary enuresis, which refers to children who have never been dry at night. If they have been dry for some time and then start wetting again, it is called secondary enuresis.

Outgrowing it or needing help

With primary enuresis the basic cause is developmental delay, which simply means that some children are a little slower than most others in being able to control their bladder during the night. Some two-year-olds have control; some eight-year-olds do not. As children grow through their primary school years, more and more of them develop bladder control. Some of them simply grow out of their difficulty, while others need help. We will look at these in more detail later.

With secondary enuresis, the cause could be no more than excessive drinking before bedtime. If it is an isolated incident, there is probably no need to worry and not much that needs to be done. However, if it begins to be a regular occurrence, then it may be wise to seek some help to overcome the problem before it damages the child's self-esteem.

Treatment

If your child is a bed-wetter, it is wise to take them to a doctor for a check-up to make sure that there is no physical cause

If you have a bed-wetter, it is wise to take the child to a doctor for a check-up to make sure that there is no physical cause. The doctor may then either undertake treatment or refer you to a pediatrician or a clinic at a children's hospital.

There are three major forms of treatment. Firstly, there is drug therapy. The child is put on a course of drugs which help to stop the wetting. Unfortunately, some children have an adverse reaction to such treatment and suffer from outbursts of anger. If you can cope with this, and the child can appreciate the dry nights, then it may be worth the effort.

Another popular treatment is the pad-and-bell method. A damp-sensitive pad is placed under the bedding, and when the pad is activated, it sets off an alarm which wakes the child, who then can get up and go to the toilet. This usually works well, especially with children trying to overcome secondary enuresis.

Behaviour therapy is also popular. With this treatment, the child's behaviour is carefully monitored so that possible causes can be identified and eliminated. If the bed-wetting is associated with certain foods, an allergy, fluid intake, or some pre-bed activity, the suspect factor can be identified and removed, along with the problem. The therapy can also be used with a reward schedule, where the child is given a reward for every dry night if certain conditions, such as no drinks after 7.30 p.m., have been complied with. Eventually it should get to the point where a dry night is its own reward, and you will not have to offer other inducements to encourage such behaviour. Until then, you may have to find some activity or treat that will help change a wet bed to a dry one.

Learning Disabilities

Learning disabilities is a general term that covers the problems encountered by children who are bright but are unable to achieve at the expected level. This achievement is usually measured in terms of their ability to read, write and spell. *Dyslexia* was a term commonly used in the past to describe this disability.

What are Learning Disabilities and Why Do They Occur?

Although much research has been done to try to identify the causes of learning disabilities, there is still no positive answer to why they occur. It could be to do with difficult births, food allergies, accidents or chemical imbalances. Until an answer is found, we are left to cope with what learning difficulties mean and what can be done for the children who suffer from them.

If your children have trouble learning to read when their classmates seem to be progressing, if they are clumsy, forgetful, put their shoes on the wrong foot, don't know their left side from their right, hate school, mistake *d* for *b* and *was* for *saw*, and say negative things about themselves all the time, then they may be suffering from a learning difficulty and could do with some help.

If your children have trouble learning to read when their classmates seem to be progressing, they may be suffering from a learning difficulty and could do with some help

> "Mum, the kids at school say I'm dumb."
>
> "What makes them say that?"
>
> "When the teacher asks me to read aloud, I always make mistakes."
>
> "Maybe I should talk to your teacher about this."

Some children need only a short period of remedial teaching to set them on the right track. For others, it can be a continuous battle to overcome their difficulties as they meet each new challenge in their life. They may always need to seek help to get them through. For these children the coding and retrieving of information does not occur in the usual way. Some can take in the information, especially if it is presented verbally, but cannot reproduce it in a written form. The patterns that are apparent to other children have to be laboriously learned by them. Others can take in and reproduce the information but they have difficulty remembering it. It is like putting something in a special spot so you will know where to find it and not being able to remember that special spot when the time comes.

How to Detect Learning Difficulties

Unfortunately for all concerned, it is often very hard to detect learning difficulties. Some teachers think a child who is not achieving reflects badly on their teaching and are inclined to believe that the child is doing better than is really the case. Worried parents may be concerned that they are pushing their child to perform and so make allowances instead of finding solutions. Children too, may be very confused and frustrated by their learning difficulties, wanting to do better and embarrassed at appearing stupid in front of their classmates when the teacher asks them to read aloud or answer a question from the board.

It is often very hard to detect learning difficulties

"Hilary, what is the answer to the question on the board?"

"I don't know, Miss."

"Surely you know the answer to that. It's simple."

"No, Miss, I don't."

"Then sit down, you silly girl."

When children show signs of having trouble learning, it is worth first having their vision and sight examined. It could simply be that they cannot see properly because they are long-sighted or short-sighted. Perhaps they have a hearing problem and need a hearing aid. If you have investigated these possibilities and there still seems to be a problem, then it is worth talking to the child's teacher. A good teacher should be able to see beyond your child's poor performance and often related disruptive behaviour and realise that something is amiss. The teacher might suggest a psychological assessment, to eliminate the possibility of emotional problems being the cause of the slow progress and determine the expected level of performance for the child.

The difficulty is, behavioural and learning problems become circular and feed one another, so that it is hard to isolate the causes from the symptoms. Is the child disruptive in class because of difficulties in learning? Or do the learning difficulties come about because the child misbehaves and does not listen to the teacher? If your child's school has a special education teacher or counsellor, that teacher may be able to monitor the child's behaviour to see what could be causing the problem or to recommend places where your child can be tested. There are several organisations, such as SPELD or A.C.L.D., that test for learning difficulties. They may also recommend the necessary remedial work and even provide such classes.

Isolating the cause from the symptoms

Child Abuse

There are people who use their parental authority or take advantage of the trusting nature of children to abuse a child, emotionally, physically or sexually. Let's consider these forms of child abuse in turn.

Emotional Abuse

Emotional abuse is the hardest to recognise and, thus, to treat. There is no obvious damage, such as bruising, but the damage done by the emotional abuse prevents the child from functioning properly. Emotional abuse can occur when a parent withholds love from a child, when the parent is inconsistent in reacting to a child's behaviour, or when the parent is cold, aggressive or verbally abusive to the child. A parent who picks on a child or who makes negative comments on the child's physical or intellectual abilities could be emotionally abusing that child.

> *"Gee, you're stupid. Don't you know anything?"*
>
> *"I'm sorry, Dad, I'll try harder. I promise."*
>
> *"There's no hope for you, you've got such a big nose."*
>
> *"My nose isn't too big."*
>
> *"Yes it is. No good ever came from anyone with a nose like that."*

All the messages we give our children stick with them. If we give them a negative message, we are burdening them with that for life. It is better to comment on the behaviour as being bad, not the individual, when you are correcting a child.

Physical Abuse

Physical abuse can range from a heavy slap to cigarette burns and worse. The difference between someone who has accidentally stepped over the line when using smacks to punish a child and a parent who systematically beats a child is sometimes hard to distinguish. Broken limbs can result from pushes or twisting. However, the real physical abuse of children is not accidental. If you are afraid you may hurt your children when you are enraged, try to remove yourself from them. Go away to another room and think through the situation that has upset you. When you have it in a better perspective and you have calmed down, then approach the child and give an appropriate punishment. Alternatively, you can talk to one of the emergency telephone counsellors available if you think you are at risk of injuring your child. The phone numbers are usually in the front of the telephone books.

If you are afraid you may hurt your children when you are enraged, try to remove yourself from them

Sexual Abuse

Sexual abuse is the form of abuse that worries most parents, especially those with daughters. However, the old idea of "stranger danger", with little children being lured into cars by raincoated men with the offer of boiled lollies, seems to be fading. Studies show that sexual abuse is usually carried out by someone known to the child, often a relative, in which case the offence is more correctly termed incest.

Nowadays, children are encouraged to follow their instincts; if they don't feel good about what an older person wants them to do, they should refuse and tell someone about it. It does not matter if the person making the advances is a stranger or not, children should feel that they have the right to refuse any advances and that there will be people who will listen to them and believe what they are saying. The "safety house" scheme offers protection to children from the advances of strangers on their way to and from school. It is a tragedy that, for some children, their own home is not a "safety house".

Sexual abuse is usually carried out by someone known to the child

Teeth

During the five-to-eleven-year period there are great changes going on in children's mouths. First they start to shed the milk teeth at the front of the mouth. This leaves them with a gap-toothed grin for a year or two between when the milk teeth fall out and the permanent teeth grow. From six they should also be growing the molars at the back of their mouths. It is very important that you take your child to the dentist regularly during this stage. The dentist can look for any abnormalities in the teeth, and can often effect simple solutions to problems which, if left unattended, could lead to huge dentist and orthodontist bills in the future.

Health

Children are prone to illness during these early school years. If they have been sheltered from common illnesses, like chicken-pox, they are at high risk of catching it once at school. Many of the old childhood illnesses, such as measles, can be avoided by immunisation. It is important that parents remember to take their children for a booster shot before they start school

Immunisation

so that the benefits of the immunisation program they underwent in infancy are continued.

Other common illnesses that affect children in this age group are middle-ear infections and tonsillitis. Sometimes these infections occur so frequently that the child requires surgery to overcome the problem.

Often children complain of a pain in the tummy. Though it may sound like a ploy to avoid school, and it often is, pain may have a physical basis. It is better to believe that the complaint is genuine and watch for other symptoms than to send a sick child off to school.

Divorce

It is an unfortunate fact that many marriages end in divorce. The effect that this has on children varies. Much depends on the tension that has existed in the household before the break-up, the animosity that remains between the parents, and the fight that may result for custody of the children.

Another factor in children's ability to cope with divorce is their age. Fives, who see things as either good or bad, may believe that they are to blame and be very upset about what has happened. They may also try to get their parents to come back together by promising to be good in the future.

Tell children what is happening and why

It is important for parents who are separating to tell their children what is happening and, as far as possible, why. Reassure them that you both still love them but that you do not want to live together any longer. Try to minimise the trauma that they are experiencing by not attacking the other parent when you have access. Instead, use that time as a chance to keep in touch with them and their interests.

> "Daddy, do you still love me?"
>
> "Of course, honey."
>
> "Why can't you live with us then? I promise I'll be good."
>
> "Well, Mummy and I decided that we didn't want to live with each other, but we still love you whether you are good or not."
>
> "I still love you, Daddy. But I wish we all could live together."

The time and energy some divorced parents spend keeping in touch with their children, even though they find it difficult to be brought into contact with their former spouse, is most impressive. Unless it only creates more fights, it is worth it for the children to have contact with both of their parents.

Talented Children

Although being or having a talented child may not seem like a problem, how parents and children cope with this talent can create problems. Talent can manifest itself in various ways — scholastic ability, sporting prowess, artistic genius — and it is best to provide an environment in which the child has the opportunity to develop any special talent to the child's desired level without being forced. Parents who are too pushy can spoil the development of a talented child. Some children withdraw into themselves, while others react by becoming show-offs.

Scholastic talent can often be nurtured within the school, especially if the school has a program for bright children which can offer them the challenges they may not receive in the ordinary classroom. Accommodating sporting ability can be more difficult, as it usually means undergoing intensive training before or after school and on the weekends. If you think that your child is enjoying the sport, in spite of all the effort, then keep up the encouragement. The development of artistic ability, whether it be in music, dance, singing, acting, painting or drawing, may be undertaken both in and out of school. For your child to achieve high levels of skill will be very time-consuming. However, many children thrive on the challenge and do not find the time that they have to devote to their interest as being a burden.

How parents and children cope with this talent can be the problem

Some well-known artistic people, like Mozart and Picasso, showed extraordinary talent at a young age and were happiest when allowed by their parents to pursue their interest. You may not know if your offspring is a budding Mozart, but at least if the child has a chance to pursue an interest, you may be surprised. Every talented person who has risen to the top in a particular field had parents. Maybe you will be able to beam with that extra bit of pride when your little genius does well. However, remember that not all geniuses are recognised in their lifetime and many suffer because of their talent. So encourage your children and give them any help they seek, but do not expect too much from them. Simply let them enjoy themselves.

10
FACING
THE
TEENS

Having enjoyed these exciting, surprising years as your children have grown from littlies in their too-big uniforms on the first day at school to adolescents about to burst out of their uniforms as they prepare for high school, you are all now facing the teens. Some parents fear that the worst is yet to come. Although adolescence may be a turbulent time, the good foundations that you have created during their earlier years will help to ease this process.

All your love, honesty, trust, humour and patience will be necessary. Unfortunately, some parents react to this period with such fear that all their former good qualities are forgotten. Instead of seeing adolescence as a time during which they are increasing the independence of their children, they react by becoming restrictive. The youngsters rebel against these restrictions, which often leads to the parents becoming more restrictive — an ever-expanding spiral of mistrust, dislike and failed communication.

Adolescence is a period of great upheaval for young people. They are having to cope with major changes in their body, which they may find confusing or embarrassing. Menstruation and nocturnal emissions can be very worrying if they have not been adequately prepared for. Think back to your own teenage years and remember how you felt about these occurrences in your life. Did you feel that your parents had let you know enough about them? If you did, then try to approach your children in the same way. If you felt confused and embarrassed, then let your children know that you want to be of more help to them, even if you still feel that your understanding is inadequate.

When they were about five, your children discovered that you were not all-knowing, as they had previously believed. It is no use pretending that you have now regained this ability simply because they are adolescents. It would be better to admit that you have had little experience of adolescence except your own, and you would like to help them through this time. This way you are entering into a partnership, you are opening up the lines of communication and allowing them to approach you about the difficulties that they are encountering.

Many parents who belong to particular groups and readily conform to the behaviour codes of these groups ridicule their adolescents for what is similar behaviour. Once you know that they will want to look as much like others as possible so as to

All your love, honesty, trust, humour and patience will be necessary

be socially acceptable, try to see it in the light of your own behaviour. If you are afraid that they will be led astray by their friends, let them know about this concern. That way you are putting the responsibility onto them not to accept such behaviour uncritically.

Instead of imposing your ideas, your dreams and your discipline onto your children, create an open atmosphere in which other ideas are acceptable, other dreams are possible, and the children can become self-disciplined. This way they are more likely to grow into the happy and productive adults you really want them to be.

FURTHER READING

Biddulph, Steve. *The Secret of Happy Children.* Bay Books, Sydney, 1984

Gessel, Arnold, Frances Ilg and Louise Bates Ames. *The Child From 5 to 10.* Hamish Hamilton, London, 1973

Gordon, Thomas. *Parent Effectiveness Training.* Wyden, New York, 1970

McCarthy, Wendy, and Sol Gordon. *Raising Your Child Responsibly in a Sexually Permissive Society.* Collins, Sydney, 1984

Pheloung, Barbara. *Help Your Child to Learn.* Tortoiseshell Press, Sydney, 1986

Singer, Dorothy and Tracey Revenson. *A Piaget Primer: How a Child Thinks.* Plume, New York, 1978

INDEX

abuse 113–15
adolescence 118–20
affection 16
aggression 50
AIDS 45–6
animals 71–2
anxiety 85
arguments 16, 18
artistic ability 117
assessment at
  school 44–5

bathing 13, 20, 23, 25, 28, 31
bed 29
bed-wetting 109–10
bicycles 73
blame 15
board games 67
books 68;
  see also reading
boys
  behaviour 49–54
  friends 53, 77, 79
breasts 32
bright children 117
broken homes 116–17
Brownies 70
bullying 18

card games 67
cartoons, television 102
choice 21
cliques 77, 80

clothes 21, 25, 30;
  see also dressing
clubs 70–1, 95–6
  secret 28, 77
coaching sport 93–4
collecting 26
competition 52, 85
computers 104–7
crafts 72–3
cricket 89
Cubs 70

dancing 74
developmental
  changes 11–35
discipline 29, 55–63
disobedience 59–61
divorce 116–17
dolls 49, 66
dreams 20
dressing 12, 23, 25, 29
dyslexia 111–12

eating 12, 18–19, 22, 25
eight-year-olds 25–7, 63, 77
eleven-year-olds 31–5
enuresis 109–10
exams 44

family 23, 30;
  see also siblings
fantasy and
  television 101

fighting 28
five-year-olds 11–17, 99–100
football 90
friends 28, 53–4, 75–82

games 24, 67
  computer 106
  see also sport
gangs 77
gender see sex differences
gifted children 87–8, 117
girls
  behaviour 49–54
  friends 53, 77, 79–80
group activities 28, 32
groups 77, 79–80
growth 10
Guides 70
gymnastics 89

handicrafts 72–3
health 115–16
homework 43–4
humour and
  television 100
hygiene 23

illness 115–16
immunisation 115–16
indecision 17
independence 32
injuries, sporting 97

leadership 32, 96
learning 40
    disabilities 111–13

manners 17, 22, 28, 30, 61–2
meals 19–20, 22;
    see also eating
menstruation 32, 119
modesty 31
money 26, 63
music 69–70

netball 90
nine-year-olds 28–9
nocturnal emissions 34, 119
normality 10
nudity 31

outdoor activities 30, 53
ownership 25

parents' associations 45
pets 71–2
physical contact 16
Piaget's theory of development 11
play 65–8;
    see also games
pocket money 63
possessions 25
pre-operational activity 11

puberty 32
pubic hair 32
punishment 29, 56–9

reading 14, 25–6, 37, 41–3, 68
relationships 22;
    see also family;
    friends
reports from school 44–5
rewards 29, 56–9

school 15, 32, 36–47, 51
school reports 44–5
Scouts 70
secret clubs 28, 77
seven-year-olds 22–4
sex
    education 16–17, 27
    on television and videos 102–4
    orientation 51
sex differences
    behavioural 49–52, 77
    physical 52–4
    stereotypes 19–20
sexual abuse 115
siblings
    as friends 78
    fighting 28
six-year-olds 17–22, 76
sleep 20
socialisation 37
spelling 26, 40–1

sport 83–97, 117
sportsmanship 90–2
stuttering 13
swimming 88–9

talented children 87–8, 117
talking 13
teachers 40, 47
teens 118–20
teeth 115
television 99–103
ten-year-olds 30, 100
tennis 89
tests, school 44
tidiness 21, 25, 29
toilet 13, 23
toys 49–50, 66–7

videos 103–4
violence 67
    on television and videos 102–4
visits 81

washing 13, 20–1, 23, 25, 28, 31
wet dreams 34, 119
winning 18, 85
writing 14, 37
written expression 40–1